Building English Vocabulary with Etymology from Latin
Book III

Peter R. Beaven

Building English Vocabulary with Etymology from Latin
Book III
Peter R. Beaven

Editor:
Katharine Webster

Contributors:
Nicia Gruener, Paulette Ghassibi
Stephen E. Stapczynski, Dominic M. Brown
S. James Boumil III, Nikhil Deliwala, Christian Waters

Revised August 27 2018

Published by
The Cheshire Press
an imprint of The Cheshire Group
Andover, MA 01810
www.cheshirepress.com

All rights reserved. No part of this book may be
reproduced or transmitted in any form or by any means
without the express written consent of the author, except for
the inclusion of quotations in reviews.

Copyright © 2005-2008 by Beaven & Associates

ISBN: 978-0-9987465-2-4

Registration Number / Date TX00068586335 / 2007-08-20

Printed in the United States of America

Beaven & Associates
3 Dundee Park, #202 A
Andover, MA 01810
www.beavenandassociates.com

Beaven, Peter R.
Building English Vocabulary with Etymology from Latin
Book III

Contents

Etymology in Building English Vocabulary..5

Lesson I
mon/monit, mons, monstro, mor, mors/mortis, mut..7
  Lesson II
nat-, nav-, neg-, nervus, nigrare..14
  Lesson III
nihil, nom-, nov-, nocturn-, nuncio...20
  Lesson IV
ocul-, odio, olere, oper-, ora-/oris, orbis, ordo, orn-, osten-................................27
  Lesson V
pax/pac-, pallo, pasc-, pass, pater, peccatum, pecunia.......................................33
  Lesson VI
pel-/puls-, pend/pens, pes/ped..39
  Lesson VII
pet-, pict-, piare, plac-, plic-...45

Test 1..51

  Lesson VIII
pon/pos/posit, pondero, pons, port/portat...55
  Lesson IX
portus, pot/poten, pota-, praeda, prehend-, press-..61
  Lesson X
prob-, puer, pugn-, pung-/punc-, puni-, puta-...67
  Lesson XI
rap-, ratio, reg-/rect-/regent, rid-/ris-..73
  Lesson XII
rog-/rogat, rota, rupt-, rus...79
  Lesson XIII
sacr-/sanctus, sagac-, sapere, salire/sult-, salis, sanguis....................................85
  Lesson XIV
satis, scintilla, scrib/script, sect, secut...91

Test 2..97

  Lesson XV
sed-/sid-, senis, sens-/sent-, simil-/simul..101
  Lesson XVI
sol, solv/solut, somn, son...107
  Lesson XVII
sparg-, spec-/spect-/spic-, spir-...113
  Lesson XVIII
sta-/stit-, stella, string-, stru/struc-, suavis, sumere..119

Lesson XIX
tact-/tang-/ting-, temere, temper-, tempore..125
Lesson XX
-tain/ten-/tin-, term-, terra..131

Test 3...137

Lesson XXI
textus, torq-/tors-/tort-, totus, tract-, trud-/trus-, turbare...141
Lesson XXII
ruptus, ultima, undare, urb-, uxor..147
Lesson XXIII
vac-/van-, vad-/vas-, valere, vendicare...153
Lesson XXIV
veni-/vent-, ventus, ver-/vera-/veri-, vorare..159
Lesson XXV
verbum, vert-/vers-, via...166
Lesson XXVI
vid-/vis-, vigilare, vinc-/vict/-vanq-..172
Lesson XXVII
viv-/vita, voc-/vox, velle/vol-, volvere..178

Test 4...184

Answer Key...188

INDEX...197

Etymology in Building English Vocabulary

The word "etymology" refers to tracing the origin and historical development of words in a language. How is a given word derived from an earlier word or words in a native or foreign language?

Just as we can "parse" or break up a sentence into parts of speech - noun, verb, adjective, adverb, etc. - so we can deconstruct a given word into its constituent meaning elements and trace their origins. For example, the word "etymology" consists of an original Greek root "etymon" - meaning "an earlier form of the same word" - and the Greek "logos" - meaning "word" or "speech", which took on the later form "-ology" - meaning "study of." So, there we have the etymology of the word "etymology."

Studying the etymology of vocabulary words reveals repeated word-formation patterns, so that we can dissect or guess the meanings of unfamiliar words based on their constituent prefixes and roots that we have encountered earlier. For example, by knowing that the prefix "pre-" means "before" or "ahead" and that "dict" is rooted in "speaking" or "saying," we can surmise that "predict" means to foretell or talk about something before it happens.

The English language is built primarily from the Anglo-Saxon (Germanic), Latin, and Greek languages. Historically, the Angles and Saxons drove out the original Celtic inhabitants and occupied Britain, and after a few brief occupations by the Roman legions, in 1066 the tribes were defeated by the Norman leader William the Conqueror, who spoke French - a language derived almost entirely from Latin. Over time, the Germanic and Latinate languages blended to become what we know as English.

Because Latin is such a fundamental basis of English and because Latin is built from a regular system of "reusable" prefixes and roots, studying these elements makes learning vocabulary more efficient. Instead of learning word meanings in isolation, by learning a standard set of Latin prefixes and common roots we can "mix and match" to learn several new words or variations. The study of etymology thus can accelerate the expansion of our vocabulary while helping us appreciate how meanings and usages have evolved.

For example, knowing that the root "gress" means "step" or "advance", and knowing a series of prefixes, we can deduce word meanings:

"ad"	= to, toward	address ("g" in "gress" becomes a "d")
"co, con"	= together	congress (movement together)
"di"	= split	digress (move away from)
"e, ex"	= out of, from	egress (way out, exit)
"in"	= in, into	ingress (way in, entrance)
"pro"	= forward, for	progress (move forward)
"re"	= back	regress (move backward)
"trans"	= across, over	transgress (move across)

So many of the words in English that relate to the intellect, words that make us pause to think and study, come from the Greek. The Roman conquest of Greece and admiration for its culture led to the incorporation of many Greek terms into Latin. So we make a point of studying Greek roots and prefixes as well. For example, the Greek root "pathos" means "feeling" or "suffering", from which come such words as:

"a"	= not	apathy (not caring)
"anti"	= against	antipathy (dislike or hostility)
"em, en"	= into, in	empathy (sharing in another's feeling)
"sym"	= together, with	sympathy (feeling sorrow for another)

In addition, there are other English words based on the same root, such as "pathetic", "pathology", "pathos", and so on.

Consider the common prefixes and cross-connections of the words below:

telecommute	micron	automaton	extrasensory	intercede
telegraph	micrograph	autobiography	extravehicular	intercept
telphone	microphone	automobile	extraterrestrial	interrupt
telescope	microscope	autograph	extraordinary	interdict
television	micromanage	autonomy	extralegal	intervene

or the roots "duc" ("lead"), "fer" ("bear, bring"), "port" ("carry") and "vers" ("turn") as below:

aqueduct	confer	report	converse
conduct	defer	deport	diverse
deduce	refer	transport	reverse
duct	transfer	teleport	adverse
ductile	prefer	airport	perverse
educate	offer	purport	obverse
induce		export	averse
produce		import	inverse
seduce		comport	transverse
viaduct		support	controversy

In the series Building English Vocabulary, a student discovers that from just one Latin or Greek root springs an exponential growth in his vocabulary, sharpened tools to articulate the written or spoken word. A broader knowledge of English leads him to greater ties to the shared cognates of French, Spanish, Italian, and Greek. A stronger grasp of English brings a deeper understanding of the plays of Shakespeare, the novels of Dickens, the essays of Emerson, the poetry of Emily Dickinson, or the oratory of Lincoln and Churchill., who as national leaders, marshaled the English language — the former to invoke peace — the latter to evoke resolve for impending battles, the victories of which in the post bellum of the twentieth century helped thrust English into its role as the lingua franca of the modern world.

Lesson I
mon/monit, mons, monstro, mor, mors/mortis, mut

MON, MONIT
to warn

MONS
mountain

MONSTRO
to show

MOR
custom

MORS, MORTIS
death

MUT
to change

---

admonish, monitor, premonition, mountebank, paramount, promontory, muster, remonstrate, morality, mores, immortal, morbid, moribund, mortal, mortify, mortuary, commute, mutable, mutate, permutation

---

Word Definitions

admonish v. to reprove gently; to caution or warn; to reprimand firmly
"Visitors are <u>admonished</u> to remove their shoes before entry into a mosque."
admonishment (n.)
admonere to urge by warning: *ad-* before + *monere* to warn

monitor v. to observe or check over a period of time
n. a person or device that watches over something or someone
"A teacher is required to <u>monitor</u> each student's academic progress.:
monitorial (adj.)
monere to warn

premonition n. a forewarning; anxiety or anticipation about the outcome of future event
"In a dream a few nights before his assassination, President Lincoln had a <u>premonition</u> of his death."
premonitory (adj.)
praemonere to forewarn: *prae* before + *monere* to warn

mountebank n. a person who deceives others through trickery
"Medicine shows in the old West featured <u>mountebanks</u> peddling phony cures."
mons, montis mountain + *in-* on, into + *banco* bench

paramount	**adj.** above all else in importance "In critical business dealings, honesty is <u>paramount</u>." *per-* by + *ad-* up to + *mons, monit* mountain
promontory	**n.** a high ridge of land or rock jutting out into a body of water; a headland; a projecting part "The Rock of Gibraltar is a <u>promontory</u> on an island located halfway between Spain and North Africa." *prominere* to jut out: *pro-* before, in front + *minere* project, overhang
muster	**v.** to summon; to gather together for inspection; to sign up for military service "A sip of wine may aid in <u>mustering</u> the courage to go on stage and speak." *muster (n.)* *monstrare* to show < *monstrum* omen < *monere* to warn
remonstrate	**v.** to express disapproval; to demonstrate reasons in protest "Her father <u>remonstrated</u> with her, but she continued to neglect her studies." *remonstration (n.), remonstrative (adj.)* *re-* back, again + *monstrare* to show, to demonstrate
morality	**n.** a set of principles of conduct; a system of ideas of right and wrong "In response to the Civil Rights movement, many Southerners argued that <u>morality</u> could not be legislated." *moralis* morality < *mos, moris* customary practices
mores	**n.** manners and customs of a particular group of people "Cannibalistic practices run contrary to Western peoples' <u>mores</u>." *mos, moris* customary practices
immortal	**adj.** living forever; unable to die; deathless "'Ozymandias' is a Keats poem reminding us that even a pharaoh is not <u>immortal</u>." *immortality (n.)* *immortalis* everlasting: *im-* not + *mortalis* mortal < *mors, mortis* death
morbid	**adj.** sickly or diseased; gloomy; preoccupied with unhealthy thoughts "Attendance at a funeral provokes <u>morbid</u> ruminations." *morbidity (n.)* *morbidus* unhealthy < *morbus* disease < *mors, mortis* death
moribund	**adj.** at the point of death; dying "Many think the Electoral College is a <u>moribund</u> institution." *moribundus* dying < *mori* to die
mortal	**adj.** subject to death; human "A <u>mortal</u> wound is one that results in death." *mortality (n.)* *mortalis* mortal < *mors, mortis* death

mortify   **v.** to humiliate or to embarrass
"Public nudity would mortify the Puritan imagination."
mortification (n.)
mortificare to kill, subdue: *mors, mortis* death + *facere* to make

mortuary   **n.** a morgue; a place where bodies are kept until burial or cremation; a funeral home
"Egypt's pyramids are mortuary temples for dead royalty."
mortuary (adj.)
mortuarius of the dead < *mortuus* dead

commute   **v.** to go from one place to another; to travel regularly between one's home and place of work; to substitute or exchange
"The murderer's death sentence was commuted by the judge to life without parole."
commuter (n.)
commutare to change, rearrange, or replace: *com-* altogether + *mutare* to move or change

mutable   **adj.** capable of or subject to change or alteration
"Mutable genes or traits are those subject to change or variability."
mutabile changeable < *mutare* to move or change

mutate   **v.** to undergo or to cause to undergo mutation (a change or alteration)
"Alchemists sought a Philosopher's Stone to mutate common metals into gold."
mutation (n.)
mutare to move or change

permutation   **n.** a complete change; a transformation; each of the possible ways in which a set or number of things can be ordered or arranged
"Five males and four females permit 20 permutations of dance pairings."
permutare to change completely: *per-* through + *mutare* to move or change

Exercise A

Fill in the blanks in the sentences below with the correct form of a word in the scroll above.

1. In Greek mythology, all the _____ gods live on Mount Olympus.

2. The firefighter had a _____ that there would be a rash of arson fires in the condemned buildings.

3. The couple had more free time, since they no longer had to _____ into the city regularly.

4. She was _____ when her boss found embarrassing photos – showing her partying at college – online at MySpace.

5. The Nacirema tribe has an interesting set of _____ that seem very primitive to most Americans.

6. Even though his father was a god, Hercules was _____ because his mother was human.

7. There are so many different Pokemon that children trying to assemble a team of them for a computer game "battle" have millions of possible _____ to choose from.

8. The special device will _____ temperature and humidity throughout the rare books library, and sound an alarm if it falls too low.

9. Almost every time my friend called up, she displayed a _____ preoccupation with the recent death of a high school acquaintance.

10. The remains of the recently dead are stored in a _____ until the funeral.

11. His boss told him that making his sales quota was of _____ importance.

12. Rather than issue a speeding ticket, the officer chose to _____ the teenage driver.

13. Smart farmers save seeds from plants that have _____ to show new, desirable genetic traits; they then use the seeds to develop hardier or tastier crops.

14. After learning that her father was _____ from pancreatic cancer, she asked the priest to administer the last rites.

15. The judge _____ with the prosecutor after learning she had withheld key evidence from the defense.

16. He tried to _____ all his strength before tackling the huge job.

17. The _____ of the times allowed the English to justify capturing Native Americans and taking them to England to teach them English, so they could act as guides for the English upon their return.

18. Human eye color is a _____ characteristic that can be determined with some degree of certainty according to the principles of genetics.

19. Historically, Jewish bankers, who were allowed to charge interest on loans, were viewed as _____ by the Christian populace.

20. The light house on the _____ was easy to identify from a great distance and protected ships from crashing into the nearby ledges.

Exercise B

Match the word with the letter of its definition.

1. ___ admonish
2. ___ commute
3. ___ immortal
4. ___ monitor
5. ___ morality
6. ___ morbid
7. ___ mores
8. ___ moribund
9. ___ mortal
10. ___ mortify
11. ___ mortuary
12. ___ mountebank
13. ___ mutable
14. ___ mutate
15. ___ muster
16. ___ paramount
17. ___ permutation
18. ___ premonition
19. ___ promontory
20. ___ remonstrate

a) a complete change, a transformation
b) to humiliate or embarrass greatly
c) at the point of death, dying
d) to observe and check over a period of time
e) capable of or subject to change
f) manners and customs of a particular people
g) to warn against something
h) a morgue
i) to undergo a change or alteration (esp. genetic)
j) above all others in importance
k) not subject to death
l) a person who deceives others
m) a projecting part
n) a set of principles of conduct
o) to travel some distance to work
p) sickly, unwholesome
q) subject to death; human
r) to gather together, collect
s) a forewarning
t) to demonstrate reasons in protest

Exercise C

Solve the crossword puzzle

Across

6. To undergo or cause to undergo a change or alteration. 8. To demonstrate reasons in protest. 11. Manners and customs of a particular group of people. 12. At the point of death, dying. 13. Capable of or subject to change or alteration. 14. Each of several possible ways in which a set or number of things can be ordered or arranged. 17. Subject to death. 18. To observe and check over a period of time. 19. A set of principles of conduct based on notions of right and wrong.

Down

1. A morgue; a place where bodies are kept until burial or cremation. 2. A high ridge of land or rock jutting out into a body of water. 3. To travel some distance between one's home and place of work on a regular basis; to substitute or exchange. 4. A forewarning; a strong feeling that something is about to happen. 5. To reprove gently; to warn; to reprimand firmly. 7. Sickly, unwholesome. 9. A person who deceives others through trickery. 10. To gather together. 12. To humiliate or embarrass. 14. Above all else in importance. 15. Unable to die.

Lesson II
nat-, nav-, neg-, nervus, nigrare

NAT-	NAV-	NEG-	NERVUS	NIGRARE
born	ship	to deny	nerve	to blacken

innate, nascent, native, nativity, prenatal, renaissance, circumnavigate, naval, nave, navigate, navigation, navy, abnegate, denigrate, negate, negation, negative, renegade, renege, enervate

Word Definitions

innate
adj. inborn; natural; inherent
"Practical experiments show that human babies have an <u>innate</u> ability to swim."
innateness (n.)
in- in + *natus* born (past participle of *nasci* to be born)

nascent
adj. just coming into existence and showing potential
"The adolescent boy's thinly sprouting facial hair was a <u>nascent</u> beard."
nascence (n.)
nasci to be born

native
adj. existing in or belonging to someone or something by nature
n. one born in or connected with a place of birth; an original inhabitant of a place; an aborigine
"Tomatoes, potatoes, cocoa, and tobacco are <u>native</u> to the Americas."
nasci to be born

nativity
n. the occasion of a person's birth; in Christianity, the birth of Jesus
"According to the Bible, three wise men attended the <u>Nativity</u>."
nativus original, native < *nasci* to be born

prenatal
adj. occurring before birth
"Good <u>prenatal</u> care is essential to the health of mother and baby."
pre- before + *nasci* to be born

renaissance
n. a rebirth; a revival of or renewed interest in something
"The artifacts unearthed in Troy sparked a <u>renaissance</u> of interest in Greek

history and culture."
re- back, again + *nasci* to be born

circumnavigate   **v.** to sail around
"European explorers circumnavigated the globe in search of new trade routes and territory."
circumnavigation (n.)
circum- around + *navigare* to sail

naval   **adj.** relating to ships or shipping; relating to a navy
"Land-locked Switzerland is not a naval power."
navis ship

nave   **n.** the central part of a church building, flanked by aisles and separated from the chancel by a step or rail
"The nave of a church got its name from its resemblance to a ship."
navis ship

navigate   **v.** to plan and direct the route or course of a ship, aircraft, car, etc; to sail; to guide; to find one's way
"Strangers have difficulty navigating Boston's winding, one-way, and poorly marked streets."
navigare to sail: *navis* ship + *agere* to drive

navigation   **n.** the art and science of guiding travel from place to place
"Prince Henry's school of navigation advanced sea exploration around southern Africa."
navigare to sail: *navis* ship + *agere* to drive

navy   **n.** a nation's warships and sea forces
"At the start of the Revolutionary War, America's navy consisted of one warship."
navis ship

abnegate   **v.** to deny the self; to renounce or reject
"The Puritans abnegated decoration for their buildings or bodies.:
abnegator (n.)
abnegare to renounce: *ab-* away from + *negare* to deny or refuse

denigrate   **v.** to tarnish the character of a person or a group of people;
to criticize unfairly; to disparage
"The politician aimed to denigrate his opponent with half-truths and rumors."
denigration (n.), denigrator (n.), denigratory (adj.)
denigrare to blacken; to defame: *de-* down, from + *nigrare* to make blacken

negate   **v.** to make ineffective or invalid; to nullify; to deny the existence of
"The seeming touchdown was negated by an offsides penalty on the play."
negare to deny or refuse

negation n. a denial, contradiction, or canceling out (of something)
"An escape clause permits the negation of a contract."
negare to deny or refuse

negative n. a statement of contradiction, denial, opposition, or refusal; an undesirable trait; a piece of film in which the colors or values are inverted
adj. pessimistic; the opposite or absence (of something); describing a number less than zero
"In radio transmissions, military personnel and airline pilots use the word 'negative' rather than 'no.'"
negativity (n.)
negare to deny

renegade n. a traitor; a deserter; an outlaw
"Geronimo refused the reservation and led his band of renegades to the mountains."
renegare to renounce: *re-* back + *negare* to deny

renege v. to go back on a promise
"The pharaoh repeatedly reneged on promises to free the Hebrew captives."
renegare: *re-* back + *negare* to deny

enervate v. to weaken; to cause to feel drained of energy
"At the end of the 10 kilometer run in the sun, the enervated runner collapsed."
enervation (n.)
enervare to weaken: *e-* without + *nervus* strength, vigor, nerve

Exercise A

Fill in the blanks in the sentences below with the correct form of a word in the scroll above.

1. Successful athletes possess _____ abilities, but practice is necessary to develop their potential.

2. Once he became president, he had to quickly flesh out his _____ vision of a more cooperative stance in foreign policy.

3. _____ people first inhabited North America at the end of the last Ice Age, or about 10,000 to 12,000 years ago.

4. With the approach of Christmas, the church set up a _____ scene outside.

5. Doctors prescribe _____ vitamins to pregnant patients to be certain the developing fetus gets the nutrients it needs.

6. At the time of the _____ in Europe, the philosophy of humanism was established and widely adopted.

7. Magellan was the first sailor to _____ the globe.

8. At the beginning of Mass, the priest processes up the _____ to the altar.

9. In 1492, Christopher Columbus sailed across the Atlantic in hopes of _____ a new trade route to India.

10. Important devices for ocean _____ include a compass and a sextant.

11. Both land and _____ battles characterized war of independence waged by the American colonists against England.

12. At one time, the _____ of the British Empire was the largest and strongest in the world.

13. A woman must _____ all luxuries in order to become a nun.

14. During recent presidential elections, the major political parties and their allies have _____ the other's candidate to gain an advantage in the polls.

15. The recent, free republication of an excellent grammar text essentially _____ the interns' efforts at creating their own.

16. A huge majority voted against the referendum, a _____ that could not be ignored.

17. Making _____ remarks to the youngster was undermining his self-confidence and self esteem.

18. A _____ former Republican, now convicted on various federal charges, has written a tell-all book about the dirty election tactics he helped develop.

19. The wealthy couple tried to _____ on their promise to send their son to Europe if he made honors at school.

20. Too many weeds will _____ the plantings in the perennial garden.

Exercise B

Match the word with the letter of its definition.

1. ___ abnegate
2. ___ circumnavigate
3. ___ denigrate
4. ___ enervate
5. ___ innate
6. ___ nascent
7. ___ native
8. ___ nativity
9. ___ naval
10. ___ nave
11. ___ navigate
12. ___ navigation
13. ___ navy
14. ___ negate
15. ___ negation
16. ___ negative
17. ___ prenatal
18. ___ renegade
19. ___ renege
20. ___ renaissance

a) the main part of a church
b) relating to ships or shipping
c) the occasion of a person's birth
d) to weaken or drain of energy
e) travel or traffic by vessels or vehicles
f) a denial
g) to sail around
h) just coming into existence
i) a rebirth (of interest in something)
j) to sail or travel
k) occurring before birth
l) all of a nation's warships
m) to renounce or reject
n) inborn
o) to make ineffective or invalid
p) a person who deserts and betrays; a rebel
q) to criticize unfairly or disparage
r) an original inhabitant of a place
s) to go back on a promise
t) a statement of opposition, denial, or contradiction

Exercise C

Across
7. To make ineffective or invalid, to nullify; to deny the existence of. 8. Inborn, natural. 10. All of a nation's war ships. 11. A traitor; a deserter; a rebel. 15. The birth of Jesus Christ. 16. To sail around. 18. To deny the self; to renounce or reject. 19. To go back on a promise.

Down
1. A contradiction or canceling out (of something). 2. Occurring before birth. 3. Just coming into existence and showing potential. 4. An undesirable trait. 5. To tarnish the character of a person or a group of people; to criticize unfairly or disparage. 6. A rebirth; a revival of or renewed interest in something. 9. The guidance of travel from place to place. 12. To plan and direct the route or course of a ship, aircraft, etc; to sail or travel; to guide. 13. Originating from a place. 14. To weaken; to drain of energy. 15. Relating to ships or shipping; relating to a navy. 17. The central part of a church building, usually separated from the chancel by a step or rail.

Lesson III
nihil, nom-, nov-, nocturn-, nuncio

NIHIL
nothing

NOM-
name

NOV-
new

NOCTURN-
night

NUNCIO
to announce

> annihilate, nihilism, cognomen, nomenclature, nominal, onomatopoeia, renowned, innovate, innovation, nova, novelty, novice, renovate, renovation, nocturnal, nocturne, announce, annunciation, renounce, renunciation

Word Definitions

annihilate
v. to destroy completely
"The Romans <u>annihilated</u> Carthage, razing the city and plowing salt into its fields."
annihilation (n.), annihilator (n.)
annihilare to reduce to nothing: *ad-* to + *nihil* nothing

nihilism
n. the rejection of all distinctions in moral or religious value and a willingness to repudiate all previous theories of morality or religious belief
"<u>Nihilism</u> can be very depressing and destructive, as illustrated in Dostoevsky's masterly novel, *The Brothers Karamazov*."
nihilist (n.)
nihil nothing

cognomen
n. a family name; a surname or last name; a nickname
"Michelangelo's lesser-know <u>cognomen</u>, or family name, was Buonarotti."
cogomen family name: *co-* together with + *nomen* name

nomenclature
n. the set of words and terms in a particular subject or field
"Each academic discipline has its specialized vocabulary, or <u>nomenclature</u>."
nomen name, noun + *calare* to call or announce

nominal	**adj.** existing in name only; very small; far below real value or cost "'To get it for a song' means to pay a <u>nominal</u> price for something." *nomen* name
onomatopoeia	**n.** a word with the quality of copying the sound associated with the designated thing, such as "buzz" or "hee-haw" "Words like 'hiss' and 'buzz,' whose sounds mimic their meaning, were created by <u>onomatopoeia</u>." *onomatopoetic (adj.)* *nom-* name + *-poios* making
renowned	**adj.** known and respected by many people; famous "Houdini was a famous magician who was particularly <u>renowned</u> as an escape artist." *renown (n.)* *re-* again (expressing intensity) + *nomen* name
innovate	**v.** to begin or to introduce something new; to change something established by introducing new methods, ideas, or products "IBM's culture of encouraging its engineers to <u>innovate</u> has won the company thousands of patents." *innovator (n.)* *innovare* to renew; to alter: *in-* into + *novare* to make new
innovation	**n.** the act of beginning or introducing something for the first time "The transistor was the crucial <u>innovation</u> that led to microchip technology." *innovare* to renew; to alter: *in-* into + *novare* to make new
nova	**n.** a star showing a sudden increase in brightness and then slowly returning to normal "Astronomers think the star of Bethlehem was a <u>nova</u>." *novus* new, young (because such stars were thought to be newly formed)
novelty	**n.** something new and unusual; the quality of being very novel "Before the assembly line and extensive paved roads made them widely available, automobiles were a <u>novelty</u>." *novel (adj.)* *novus* new, young
novice	**n.** someone who is beginning; a person who is new to and inexperienced in a job or situation; a rookie "He was a <u>novice</u> at golf, so he had a high handicap." *novus* new, young
renovate	**v.** to repair, to modernize, or to restore something to its original condition "The decision to <u>renovate</u> the bathroom required them to buy new fixtures and tiles." *renovator (n.)* *renovare* to make new again: *re-* again + *novare* to make new

renovation	**n.** a restoration; a rebuilding to modernize "As part of extensive <u>renovations</u>, the museum added a new gallery and replaced the carpeting throughout." *renovare* to make new again: *re-* again + *novare* to make new
nocturnal	**adj.** occurring or active at night "Owls and bats are <u>nocturnal</u> creatures who do most of their hunting at night and sleep during the day." *nocturnus* of the night < *nox, noctis* night
nocturne	**n.** a painting of a night scene (in art); a short composition of a romantic or moody nature (in music) "Rembrandt's dark canvas 'The Night Watch' is an example of a <u>nocturne</u>." *nocturnus* of the night < *nox, noctis* night
announce	**v.** to make known publicly "'The Wedding March' traditionally <u>announces</u> the bride's procession down the aisle toward the altar." *announcement (n.)* *annuntiare* to announce < *nuncio* messenger, report
annunciation	**n.** a proclamation or announcement "Gabriel's <u>annunciation</u> informed Mary of Christ's incarnate conception." *annunciate (v.)* *annuntiare* to announce < *nuncio* messenger, report
renounce	**v.** to give up; to relinquish; to formally declare one's abandonment of; to refuse to recognize any longer "St. Augustine <u>renounced</u> relations with women later in his life." *renouncement (n.), renouncer (n.), renounceable or renunciable (adj.)* *renuntiare* to reject: *re-* back + *nuntiare* to announce or warn
renunciation	**n.** the giving up of a title or position; the act of renouncing; the abandonment of a right or position "Edward's <u>renunciation</u> of the throne to marry a divorcée made Elizabeth queen." *renunciate (v.)* *renuntiare* to reject: *re-* back + *nuntiare* to announce or warn

Exercise A

Fill in the blanks in the sentences below with the correct form of a word in the scroll above.

1. Whether or not the European colonists intended to _____ the Native American population, they nearly succeeded: not with arms, but with the diseases they brought with them, especially smallpox.

2. The philosophy teachers voted not to include _____ in the curriculum, because they felt it could encourage students to abandon all morality.

3. Many _____ arose from an ancestor's trade or name, such as "Smith" for blacksmith, or "Jacobson" for "son of Jacob."

4. Terms like "treble clef" and "crescendo" come from musical _____.

5. The community center charges a _____ fee to local groups wishing to meet there, and charges nothing for use by nonprofits.

6. "Splash" and "smack" are examples of words formed by _____.

7. She was _____ for her large, tasty vegetables, which won first prize each fall at the county fair.

8. To improve on an existing invention is one feat; to _____ a completely new device is quite another.

9. Wang prized _____ and his company won many important patents in the nascent computer industry, yet often failed to capitalize on them in the marketplace.

10. Astronomers first believed _____ were new stars, but later learned they are stars that suddenly increase in brightness, then slowly return to normal.

11. Elaborate full-color tattoos, once a _____, are now as commonplace as pierced ears.

12. At ski resorts, the slopes that are labeled "_____" are considerably easier and less steep than those designated "intermediate" or "black diamond."

13. Work to _____ the Statue of Liberty began in time to prevent further deterioration of the national landmark.

14. The _____ of the Red House in Marshfield, Massachusetts – the oldest, continually lived-in house in New England – was a labor of love.

15. Few of Claude Monet's paintings were _____, as he used vibrant colors and mostly painted on sunny days.

16. Animals that are more active at night than during the day are _____.

17. The reporter will _____ the winners of the contest on the evening news.

18. The _____ of the birth of Christ was a beloved subject of medieval and Renaissance painters.

19. The news that the king was going to _____ his title stunned the world.

23

20. His _____ of meat helped lessen his gout.

Exercise B

Match the word with the letter of its definition.

1. ___ annihilate
2. ___ announce
3. ___ annunciation
4. ___ cognomen
5. ___ innovate
6. ___ innovation
7. ___ nihilism
8. ___ nocturnal
9. ___ nocturne
10. ___ nomenclature
11. ___ nominal
12. ___ nova
13. ___ novelty
14. ___ novice
15. ___ onomatopoeia
16. ___ renovate
17. ___ renovation
18. ___ renounce
19. ___ renowned
20. ___ renunciation

a) to begin or introduce something new
b) very small, of minimal value
c) a restoration
d) to completely destroy
e) a moody or romantic piece of music
f) to give up, to relinquish
g) a proclamation or announcement
h) something new and unusual
i) the formation of a word from a sound associated with the thing it signifies
j) a philosophy rejecting all religious and moral principles
k) the giving up of a title or position
l) to make known publicly
m) a new invention or way of doing something
n) to restore to a good state of repair
o) a family name; a surname; a nickname
p) a beginner
q) occurring or active at night
r) the set of terms used in a particular field
s) famous
t) a star showing a sudden increase in brightness and then slowly returning to normal

Exercise C

Solve the crossword puzzle

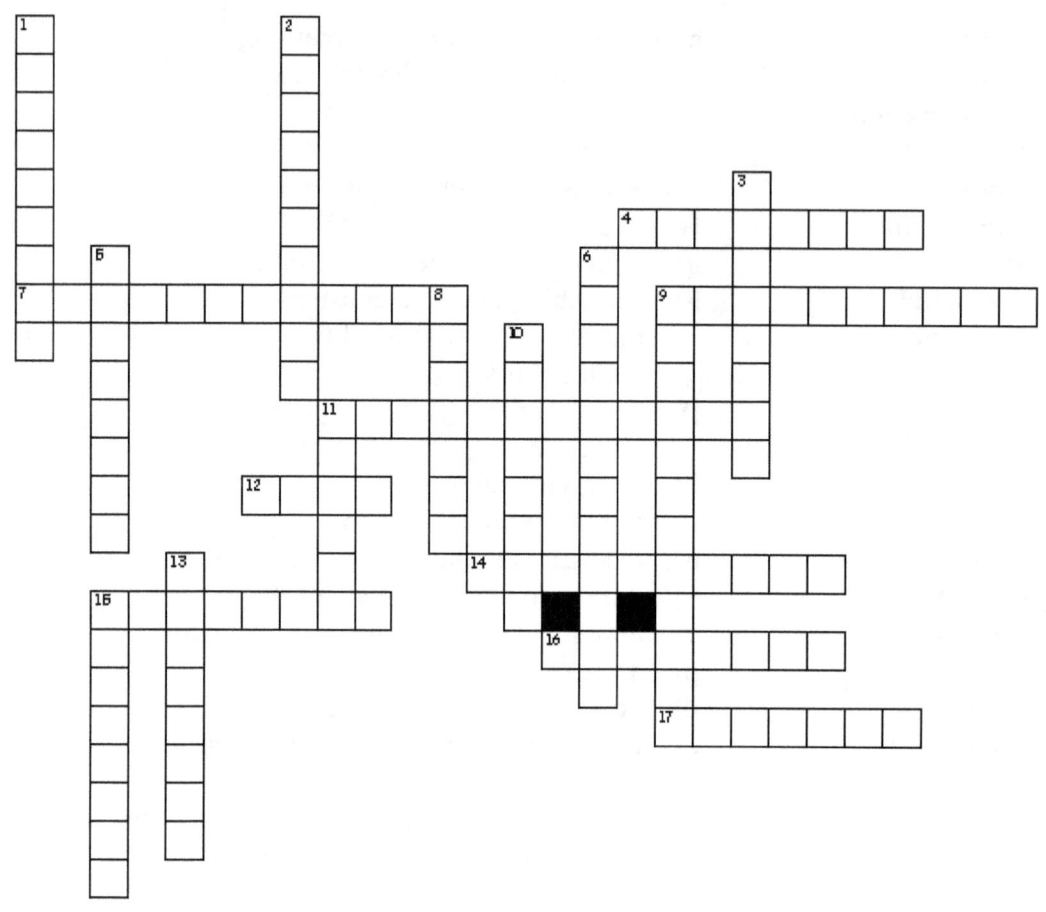

Across
4. To repair or restore something to its original condition. 7. A proclamation. 9. A restoration. 11. The set of terms used in a particular field. 12. A star showing a sudden increase in brightness, then slowly returning to normal. 14. To begin or introduce something for the first time. 15. Known and respected by many people. 16. The rejection of all religious and moral principles. 17. Existing in name only; very small, far below real value or cost.

Down
1. Occurring or active at night. 2. To completely destroy. 3. A family name, surname, or nickname. 5. To make known publicly. 6. A word with the quality of sounding like the thing designated. 8. Something new and unusual; the quality of being novel. 9. The giving up of a title or position; the action of renouncing; the abandonment of a right or position. 10. A painting of a night scene. 11. A beginner; a person who is new to and inexperienced in a job or situation. 13. To begin or introduce something new; to change something established by introducing new methods, ideas, or products. 15. To give up, to relinquish; to formally declare one's abandonment of; to refuse to recognize any longer.

Lesson IV

ocul-, odio, olere, oper-, ora-/oris, orbis,
ordo, orn-, osten-

| *OCUL-* | *ODIO* | *OLERE* |
| eye | to hate | smell |

| *OPER-* | *ORA-/ORIS* | *ORBIS* |
| to work | to speak/mouth | circle |

| *ORDO* | *ORN-* | *OSTEN-* |
| order | to decorate, adorn | to exhibit |

*oculist, odious, olfactory, redolent, operate, oracle,
orator, orifice, oration, orb, orbit, inordinate, insubordinate, ordain,
ordinance, ornament, ornate, ostensible, ostentatious*

Word Definitions

oculist n. a person who treats diseases or defects of the eye
"Ben Franklin proved himself an amateur <u>oculist</u> with his invention of bifocals."
oculus eye

odious adj. extremely unpleasant; repulsive; hateful
"Cleaning a septic tank is an <u>odious</u> task, even for some professionals."
odiousness (n.)
odio to hate

olfactory adj. relating to the sense of smell
"Most of the sense of taste actually derives from the <u>olfactory</u> organ – the nose."
olfacere to smell (a variant of *olere* to smell)

redolent adj. fragrant; aromatic; reminiscent
"Grandmother's attic is <u>redolent</u> of mothballs and the past."

| | *redolence (n.)* |
| | *redolere* to give off a scent; odorous: *re-* back, again + *olere* to smell |

operate   **v.** to function or to control the function of; to manage or to run; to perform surgery
"Mob bosses stereotypically <u>operate</u> out of pizza parlors and bars."
operator (n.)
operari to work < *opus, operis* work

oracle   **n.** a priest or priestess acting as a medium for divine advice or prophecy; an infallible authority
"Oedipus relied on the <u>oracle</u> of Delphi to reveal his fate."
orare to speak or pray

orator   **n.** a proficient public speaker
"With his masterful speech, <u>orator</u> Daniel Webster overcame the Devil himself."
orate (v.), oration (n.)
orator speaker

oration   **n.** a formal speech
"Hale's <u>oration</u> at Gettysburg lasted some two hours, before Lincoln rose to speak for less than five minutes."
orare to speak or pray

orifice   **n.** an opening; a bodily opening, such as the mouth
"The Cyclops rolled away a large rock to reveal the <u>orifice</u> of his cave."
orificium opening: *os, oris* mouth + *facere* to make

orb   **n.** a spherical object or shape
"The planets are <u>orbs</u> regularly circling a central sun."
orbis circle, sphere

orbit   **n.** the regularly repeated circular or elliptical course of a celestial object; a circle (of friends)
v. to revolve around
"Wealthy families rarely admit the financially inferior into their social <u>orbit</u>."
orbis circle, sphere

inordinate   **adj.** unusually large; excessive
"Any one person's chance of winning the lottery jackpot is <u>inordinately</u> small."
inordinatus occurring irregularly: *in-* not + *ordinatus* set in order; regulated

insubordinate   **adj.** defiant of authority; disobedient
"Defiance of a direct order from a superior constitutes <u>insubordinate</u> behavior."
in- not + *sub-* under + *ordinatus* set in order; regulated

ordain   **v.** to confer holy orders on; to order or appoint officially
"After years of study in a seminary, a theologian may be <u>ordained</u> as a

	minister." *ordinare* to arrange, to rank < *ordo, ordinis* order
ordinance	**n.** an authoritative order; a municipal rule or local regulation "The town has <u>ordinances</u> prohibiting shirtless, barefoot customers in stores." *ordinare* to arrange, to rank < *ordo, ordinis* order
ornament	**n.** an object that decorates something **v.** to beautify or decorate something "A car's hood <u>ornament</u> usually shows the car maker's symbol." *ornare* to adorn; to honor
ornate	**adj.** elaborately or highly decorated "Tutankhamen's gold sarcophagus is <u>ornate</u>, with enamel inlay and precious jewels." *ornare* to adorn; to honor
ostensible	**adj.** apparently true, but not necessarily so "The <u>ostensible</u> reason he gave for being late turned out to be a fib." *ostendere* to reveal or display
ostentatious	**adj.** characterized by pretentious or showy display; designed to impress "Gold flatware, crystal goblets, and damask napkins made for an <u>ostentatious</u> table." *ostendere* to reveal or display

Exercise A

Fill in the blanks in the sentences below with the correct form of a word in the scroll above.

1. _____, he went to the convention in Hawaii to update his professional skills, but he spent most of his time on the beach.

2. The _____ soldier was assigned latrine duty after defying his sergeant repeatedly.

3. At high school graduations, one student _____ is typically the valedictorian and the other is the salutatorian.

4. In accordance with the town's _____, cars parked in fire lanes or next to hydrants were towed immediately.

5. The couple hung the _____ crystal chandelier in their window where the entire neighborhood could see it.

6. The six week-old milk was _____ of sour vinegar.

7. If she's accumulated an _____ amount of clothes, she should donate some to the Salvation Army.

8. The kangaroo's pouch is an _____ in which she carries and nurses her newborn joeys.

9. The surgeon was ready to _____, but the anesthesiologist was late.

10. In extreme cases of conjunctivitis, commonly known as pink eye, a patient may have to see an _____.

11. The _____ nerve is connected to the most primitive part of our brain, indicating the importance to our ancestors' survival of a good sense of smell.

12. Families use garlands of popcorn, gingerbread people, candy canes and other _____ to decorate their Christmas trees.

13. Hillary Clinton's _____ was a highlight of the Democratic convention.

14. A planet may be referred to as an _____, due to its spherical shape.

15. In *Ulysses and the Golden Fleece*, Ulysses visits the _____ to learn his destiny.

16. The bishop is preparing to _____ several new priests.

17. The bully's _____ name-calling infuriated his victim.

18. Students studying cosmology learn to calculate the path of a planet, known as its _____.

19. The marble statue was especially _____ and delicate, and several small embellishments broke off during the move.

Exercise B

Match the word with the letter of its definition:

1. ___ inordinate
2. ___ insubordinate
3. ___ oculist
4. ___ odious
5. ___ olfactory
6. ___ operate
7. ___ oracle
8. ___ orator
9. ___ oration
10. ___ orb
11. ___ orbit
12. ___ ordain
13. ___ ordinance
14. ___ orifice
15. ___ ornament
16. ___ ornate
17. ___ ostensible
18. ___ ostentatious
19. ___ redolent

a) strongly suggestive of; smelling of
b) an opening (especially of the body)
c) a person who treats diseases or defects of the eye
d) a decorative object
e) the elliptical course of a celestial body; a social sphere
f) to order or appoint officially
g) unusually large (in quantity)
h) to function; to manage or run
i) an infallible authority; a seer
j) apparently true, but not necessarily so
k) a spherical object or shape
l) defiant of authority
m) relating to the sense of smell
n) characterized by pretentious display; showy
o) an authoritative order; a local law
p) elaborately or highly decorated
q) a formal speech
r) extremely unpleasant; hateful
s) a proficient public speaker

Exercise C

Solve the crossword puzzle.

Across

1 A spherical object or shape 3 Extremely unpleasant; repulsive; hateful 5 To confer holy orders on; to order or appoint officially 7 Fragrant; aromatic; reminiscent 9 An opening; a bodily opening, such as the mouth 11 A formal speech 12 Unusually large; excessive 13 Relating to the sense of smell 14 Defiant of authority; disobedient 15 A person who treats diseases or defects of the eye

Down

1 An object that decorates something 2 A priest acting as a medium for divine advice or prophecy 3 To function or to control the function of 4 Elaborately or highly decorated 5 A proficient public speaker 6 The regularly repeated circular or elliptical course of a celestial object 8 An authoritative order; a municipal rule or local regulation 9 Designed to impress 10 Apparently true, but not necessarily so

Lesson V

pax/pac-, pallo, pasc-, pass, pater, peccatum, pecunia

PAX, PAC- peace	**PALLO** to long for	**PASC-** to feed	**PASS** to feel, to suffer
PATER father	**PECCATUM** sin	**PECUNIA** money	

appease, pacifist, pacify, pall, palliate, pallid, pastoral, repast, impassioned, impassive, passionate, paternity, patrimony, patriotism, patron, patronize, impeccable, peccadillo, impecunious, pecuniary

Word Definitions

appease
v. to soothe or calm; to placate by giving in to demands
"The Aztecs sacrificed thousands of prisoners to <u>appease</u> their bloodthirsty gods."
appeasement (n.), appeaser (n.)
ad- to, at + *pax, pacis* peace

pacifist
n. a person who supports peace and opposes war; a practitioner of non-violence
"Gandhi, a <u>pacifist</u>, was revolted by the prospect of an India-Pakistan war."
pacificare to pacify; to make peace: *pac-* peace + *facere* to make or do

pacify
v. to quiet; to bring peace to or tame; to put down a rebellion
"Because he was unable to <u>pacify</u> the savage Picts, Hadrian built a wall along the Scottish border."
pacifier (n.)
pacificare to pacify; to make peace: *pac-* peace + *facere* to make or do

pall
n. a covering that darkens or obscures; an atmosphere of gloom or fear; a coffin covering
"Los Angeles is almost continuously covered in a yellow <u>pall</u> of pollution."
pallium a covering or cloak

palliate	**v.** to relieve or to mitigate; to disguise "Hospice workers aim to palliate the suffering associated with terminal illness, not to cure disease." *palliative (adj.)* *palliare* to cloak or disguise < *pallium* a covering or cloak
pallid	**adj.** pale (of a person's complexion); lacking intensity of color; lacking in radiance or vitality; dull "The moribund patient looked more pallid each day." *pallere* to be pale; to fade
pastoral	**adj.** pertaining to shepherds or to the countryside "Wordsworth's poems often feature pastoral settings." *pastor, pastoris* shepherd or herdsman < *pascere* to feed and *pascua* pasture
repast	**n.** a meal "A roast turkey is the standard centerpiece of the Thanksgiving repast." *re-* again (expressing intensity) + *pascere* to feed
impassioned	**adj.** filled with or showing great emotion "Patrick Henry spoke the impassioned words: 'Give me liberty or give me death!'" *passus* (past participle of the verb *patior* to suffer; to feel)
impassive	**adj.** not feeling or showing emotion "The Stoics strove to show neither pain nor pleasure, but remain impassive." *im-* not + *passus* (past participle of the verb *patior* to suffer; to feel)
passionate	**adj.** having or showing strong feelings; unstinting in devotion "Anthony and Cleopatra pursued a passionate love affair before committing suicide." *patior* to suffer; to feel
paternity	**n.** fatherhood; paternal descent "Brutus's paternity is uncertain; he may have been Caesar's bastard son." *pater, patris* father
patrimony	**n.** an inheritance; heritage (from a male ancestor) "Typically, the patrimony of the eldest son was his father's estate, farm, or business, while younger brothers were apprenticed out or educated for a different livelihood." *pater, patris* father
patriotism	**n.** the love of one's country (or fatherland) and the willingness to defend it "American flags and veterans' parades are displays of patriotism." *patriot (n.)* *pater, patris* father
patron	**n.** a person who gives financial support; a customer "Theater patrons are asked to switch off cell phones during performances."

	patronage (n.) *pater, patris* father
patronize	**v.** to act as a patron; to support something; to treat condescendingly "The doctor took a <u>patronizing</u> tone when lecturing his patient, a two-pack-a-day smoker." *pater, patris* father
impeccable	**adj.** flawless; perfect; in accordance with the highest standards "The credentials of the Supreme Court candidate were <u>impeccable</u>." *in-* not + *peccabilis* sinful < *peccare* to sin
peccadillo	**n.** a small sin or fault "Nodding off at the table is more a minor <u>peccadillo</u> than a sin." *peccare* to sin
impecunious	**adj.** having little or no money "Most bag ladies are <u>impecunious</u>, but a few are mere eccentrics." *impecuniosity (n.), impecuniousness (n.)* *im-* not + *pecunia* money, property
pecuniary	**adj.** pertaining to money "A <u>pecuniary</u> reward was offered for information leading to the suspect's arrest." *pecunia* money, property

Exercise A

Fill in the blanks in the sentences below with the correct form of a word in the scroll above.

1. The _____ actor drew a standing ovation for his performance as Othello.

2. She had a _____ as well as an emotional interest in the success of her daughter's business, as she had invested much of her life's savings in it.

3. Lorenzo de Medici was a _____ of the arts during the Renaissance, supporting painters such as Leonardo da Vinci and Michelangelo.

4. Find a career that involves something about which you are _____ and you will never have to work a day in your life.

5. A person who joins a group that opposes all wars is a _____.

6. Although she lived in Greenwich Village, she loved to paint _____ scenes, based on her memories of growing up in rural Vermont.

7. The only surviving heir anticipated receiving his _____ as soon as the estate was settled.

8. To _____ business owners, the city built a large parking garage before starting a messy construction project on Main Street.

9. His flirtations and other _____ exasperated his wife.

10. During the American Revolution, Paul Revere and his midnight ride became a classic symbol of American _____.

11. When the jury announced its guilty verdict, the suspect remained _____, although his girlfriend began sobbing.

12. The midday _____ was extremely satisfying and filling, so afterwards the masons decided to take a siesta.

13. The mother gave a cookie to her fretful child to _____ him, while they waited for the waitress to take their orders.

14. Henry Higgins taught and coached Eliza Doolittle until her diction, dress, and manners were _____.

15. When she came back from sick leave, she still looked _____.

16. The responsibilities that come with _____ shocked the new father.

17. Doctors often cannot "fix" back pain, but can _____ the patient's suffering while rest effects a cure.

18. Before Staples drove Jim's Family Business Warehouse into bankruptcy, Dr. Friedman _____ the small business because Jim was a family friend.

19. The news that two seniors had died in a drunken driving accident the previous night cast a _____ over graduation.

20. The man became _____ after he gambled away his savings in Las Vegas.

36

Exercise B

Match the word with the letter of its definition.

1. ___ appease
2. ___ impassioned
3. ___ impassive
4. ___ impeccable
5. ___ impecunious
6. ___ pacifist
7. ___ pacify
8. ___ pall
9. ___ palliate
10. ___ pallid
11. ___ pastoral
12. ___ repast
13. ___ passionate
14. ___ paternity
15. ___ patrimony
16. ___ patriotism
17. ___ patron
18. ___ patronize
19. ___ peccadillo
20. ___ pecuniary

a) a meal
b) not feeling or showing emotion
c) pertaining to money
d) to quiet; to put down a rebellion
e) lacking in radiance or vitality
f) to relieve or disguise
g) having or showing unstinting devotion
h) to soothe or calm
i) flawless; perfect
j) support for one's country
k) an atmosphere of gloom or fear
l) to support something (esp. the arts)
m) a person who supports peace and opposes war
n) a small sin or fault
o) filled with or showing great emotion
p) a person who gives financial support
q) having little or no money
r) fatherhood; paternal descent
s) pertaining to shepherds or the countryside
t) an inheritance or heritage (from a male ancestor)

Exercise C

Solve the crossword puzzle:

Across
4. Pertaining to money. 5. Having little or no money. 6. A person who gives financial support (to a person, organization, or cause). 7. Pale (of a complexion); lacking intensity of color; lacking in radiance or vitality; dull. 9. An inheritance or heritage (from a male ancestor). 11. To relieve or mitigate; to disguise. 12. Pertaining to shepherds or the countryside. 13. To act as a patron; to support something; to act condescending. 17. Flawless, perfect; in accordance with the highest standards. 19. To make quiet; to bring peace to.

Down
1. A small sin or fault. 2. Having or showing unstinting devotion. 3. Fatherhood; paternal descent. 8. A covering that darkens or obscures, an atmosphere of gloom or fear; a coffin covering. 9. Love of one's country and a willingness to defend it. 10. Filled with or showing great emotion. 14. Not feeling or showing emotion. 15. A person who supports peace and opposes war. 16. A meal. 18. To soothe or calm; to placate (someone) by acceding to their demands.

Lesson VI
pel-/puls-, pend/pens, pes/ped

PEL-, PULS- to drive	PEND, PENS to hang, to weigh	PES, PED foot

compel, compulsion, expel, propel, propeller, repel, appendix, impending, penchant, pendant, pending, propensity, expedient, expedite, impediment, pediment, pedal, pedestrian, pedigree, pedometer

Word Definitions

compel
v. to force or oblige to do something
"Concentration camp inmates were <u>compelled</u> to perform hard labor."
 compelling (n.)
compellere to drive together; to force: *com-* together + *pellere* to drive

compulsion
n. an irresistible urge to behave in a certain way
"A <u>compulsion</u> to repeatedly wash one's hands may originate in an obsession with cleanliness."
compellere to drive together; to force: *com-* together + *pellere* to drive

expel
v. to force or drive out
"A touch-me-not plant <u>expels</u> its seeds when touched or brushed against."
expellere to drive out or banish; to reject: *ex-* out + *pellere* to drive

propel
v. to drive or push forward
"The so-called people mover efficiently <u>propels</u> travelers through airport corridors."
propellere to drive forward: *pro-* forward + *pellere* to drive

propeller
n. a fan-like device that drives an aircraft or boat by pushing back air or water
"A jet's turbine engines outperform an airplane's <u>propellers</u>."
propellere to drive forward: *pro-* forward + *pellere* to drive

repel
v. to drive or to force back or away
"DEET is the recommended skin chemical to use to <u>repel</u> mosquitoes."
repellere to drive back or away; to fend off: *re-* back + *pellere* to drive

39

appendix	**n.** an attachment or addition; an apparently useless attachment to the intestine "The appendix of this book consists of answer keys." *appendere* to hang from or suspend: *a-* from + *pendere* to hang
impending	**adj.** about to happen; looming "The darkening clouds indicated an impending thunderstorm." *impendere* to overhang; to threaten: *im-* against + *pendere* to hang
penchant	**n.** a strong inclination or liking "The musically gifted youngster showed a penchant for the piano." *pendere* to hang
pendant	**n.** an ornament hanging from something else (esp. a necklace or chain) "The rapper wore a diamond-studded crucifix pendant on a gold chain." *pendere* to hang
pending	**adj.** not yet decided or settled "A pending patent is one that's been applied for, but is awaiting approval." *pendere* to hang
propensity	**n.** an inclination or tendency "Falstaff had a propensity for drink, particularly for sack – a sherry-like wine." *propendere* to hang down; to be inclined: *pro-* forward, down + *pendere* to hang
expedient	**adj.** convenient and practical, although possibly improper or immoral "Today's youth find e-mail more expedient than letter-writing." *expedire* to set free (orig. by freeing the feet); to loosen: *ex-* out + *pes, pedis* foot
expedite	**v.** to cause to be accomplished more quickly "First class postage, rather than book rate, will expedite delivery." *expedire* to set free (orig. by freeing the feet); to loosen: *ex-* out + *pes, pedis* foot
impediment	**n.** a hindrance or obstacle "A lisp or a stutter is a speech impediment." *impedire* to hinder or obstruct: *im-* not, against + *pes, pedis* foot
pediment	**n.** a gable surmounting the façade of a building in the Greek style; a gently sloping rock formation "The triangular roof support of the Parthenon exemplifies a pediment." *pes, pedis* foot
pedal	**n.** a foot-operated lever "A foot pedal operated the spinning wheel and the sewing machine." *pes, pedis* foot
pedestrian	**n.** a person traveling by foot; common, ordinary "Blue-collar workers have pedestrian occupations requiring no higher

education."
pedester going on foot; of foot-soldiers; commonplace

pedigree   n. a lineage; a genealogical table
"A mutt is a dog of unknown or mixed pedigree."
ped- foot + *grue* crane (from the "crane's foot" marks on a genealogy chart)

pedometer   n. a device that measures how far one has walked
"Most waist-clip pedometers measure distance by calculating two strides for each bump of the wearer's hip."
pes, ped- foot

Exercise A

Fill in the blanks in the sentences below with the correct form of a word in the scroll above:

1. A _____ in a crosswalk has the right of way.

2. Due to problems with the real estate agent, the sale of the house was still _____ six weeks after an offer was made.

3. When the boat hit the rock, the _____ was damaged beyond repair.

4. The architect noted that the present _____ on the building was not original and that something more appropriate should be selected for the renovation.

5. In the experiment, the magnets _____ each other because the positive poles were facing each other.

6. Even though the detectives thought it would be more _____ to extricate the papers from the safe right away, they decided to wait for a search warrant.

7. Unusual behavior in animals can be a warning of _____ natural disasters, such as earthquakes and tsunamis.

8. Successful television series use plot twists and cliffhangers to _____ viewers to tune in week after week.

9. The bicycle repairman installed new _____ without straps.

10. The principal threatened to _____ the disruptive and sometimes violent child.

11. The Osbornes have a _____ for fancy cars.

12. He had a _____ to lie when caught doing something naughty.

13. The tree knocked down by the tornado was an _____ to ambulances and fire trucks trying to reach the scene of the disaster.

14. Robin Hood was a mythical figure who felt an ethical _____ to steal from the rich and give to the poor.

15. The _____ to the *Lord of the Rings* trilogy provides important information about the lineage of the main characters.

16. The aspiring marathon runner decided to invest in a _____ .

17. She told the jeweler that she was looking for a suitable _____ to hang from her antique gold chain.

18. Even though he cut the engine, the car's momentum _____ them into the ditch.

19. To _____ the mortgage loan, the banker offered to oversee the transaction personally.

20. Marilyn is looking for a Lhasa Apso with a good _____ , because she wants to breed show dogs.

Exercise B

Match the word with the letter of its definition.

1. ___ appendix
2. ___ compel
3. ___ compulsion
4. ___ expedient
5. ___ expedite
6. ___ expel
7. ___ impediment
8. ___ impending
9. ___ pedal
10. ___ pedestrian
11. ___ pedigree
12. ___ pediment
13. ___ pedometer
14. ___ penchant
15. ___ pendant
16. ___ pending
17. ___ propel
18. ___ propeller
19. ___ propensity
20. ___ repel

a) a device that measures walking or running distance
b) a device that drives an aircraft or boat
c) a gable surmounting a building's façade
d) to force or drive out
e) a strong inclination
f) a lineage
g) to cause to be accomplished more quickly
h) an attachment or addition
i) to force or oblige to do something
j) a foot-operated lever
k) not yet decided or settled
l) a hindrance or obstacle
m) an inclination or tendency
n) to drive or push forward
o) about to happen
p) an ornament suspended from something
q) to drive away or force back
r) convenient and practical, but not necessarily moral
s) a person traveling on foot
t) an irresistible urge to behave in a certain way

Exercise C

Solve the crossword puzzle:

Across
1. A hindrance or obstacle. 4. To hasten; to cause to be accomplished more quickly. 7. A device for pushing forward an aircraft or boat. 9. A device that measures how far one has walked or run. 11. A person traveling by foot. 13. A gable surmounting the façade of a building in the Greek style; a gently sloping rock formation. 14. About to happen; looming. 17. An attachment or addition; an apparently useless attachment to the intestine. 18. To force or oblige to do something.

Down
2. A lineage; a genealogical table. 3. To drive or force back or away. 5. An irresistible urge to behave in a certain way. 6. To force or push out. 7. An inclination or tendency. 8. Not yet decided or settled. 10. Convenient and practical although possibly improper or immoral. 12. A foot-operated lever. 13. An ornament suspended from something else. 15. To drive or push forward. 16. A strong inclination.

Lesson VII
pet-, pict-, piare, plac-, plic-

PET-
to seek

PICT-
to paint

PIARE
to appease

PLAC-
to please

PLIC-
to fold

appetite, compete, competitor, petition, petulant, depict, pictograph, expiate, impious, piety, pittance, complacent, complaisant, implacable, placate, placid, complicit, complicity, duplicity, implicit

Word Definitions

appetite
n. an instinctive physical desire, especially for food or drink
"The bone-weary soldiers had no appetite for battle that day."
appetize (v.)
appetere to desire; to strive for: *ad-* toward + *petere* to seek; to assail

compete
v. to strive against another to attain a goal
"Rival television shows in the same time slot compete for audience share."
competitive (adj.), competition (n.)
competere to strive together: *com-* together + *petere* to seek; to assail

competitor
n. a rival
"The tortoise and the hare were seemingly ill-matched competitors."
competere to strive together: *com-* together + *petere* to seek; to assail

petition
n. a formal request to a superior authority for a right or benefit
"The Magna Carta ensued from the nobles' petition for rights from King John."
petere to seek

petulant
adj. irritable or ill-tempered, especially about trivial matters
"The spoiled toddler became petulant when asked to share her toys."
petulans impudent; unruly < *petere* to seek; to assail

depict	**v.** to represent in a picture, sculpture, photo, words, etc. "The face of George Washington is <u>depicted</u> on both the quarter and the dollar bill." *depiction (n.)* *depictus* painted or pictured (past participle of the verb *depingere*: *de-* from + *pingere* to paint)
pictograph	**n.** a picture representing a word or idea "A drawing of a leaf next to a bee might be a <u>pictograph</u> for the word 'belief.'" *pictus* painted or pictured (past participle of the verb *pingere* to paint)
expiate	**v.** to make amends for; to atone "He performed 40 hours of community service to <u>expiate</u> his vandalism." *expiare* to expiate; to atone for: *ex-* out of + *piare* to appease
impious	**adj.** lacking reverence or respect "Joan of Arc was burned at the stake for her <u>impious</u> act of donning men's clothing." *impiety (n.)* *im-* not + *pius* pious < *piare* to appease (the gods)
piety	**n.** reverence or devotion to a god or gods "A pilgrimage to Mecca is a prescribed act of <u>piety</u> for all Muslims." *pious (adj.)* *pius* pious < *piare* to appease (the gods)
pittance	**n.** a small amount of money (from the small allowance of food in a monastery) "The price of a meal at McDonald's is a <u>pittance</u> compared to the tab at the Four Seasons." *piatus* appeased (past participle of the verb *piare*, to appease [the gods])
complacent	**n.** smug and self-satisfied "The grasshopper's <u>complacent</u> attitude toward work during the summer left it ill-prepared for winter." *complacence (n.)* *complacitus* pleased (past participle of the verb *complacere* to please or win the sympathy of: *com-* together + *placere* to please; to appease)
complaisant	**adj.** willing to please; cheerfully obliging "Their nanny was a <u>complaisant</u> Salvadoran girl who also did housework." *complaisance (n.)* *complacere* to please or win the sympathy of: *com-* together + *placere* to please; to appease)
implacable	**adj.** impossible to satisfy or appease "William Jennings Bryant was an <u>implacable</u> foe of evolutionary theory." *implacability (n.)* *im-* not + *placitus* pleased (past participle of the verb *placere* to please; to appease)

placate	**v.** to calm; to pacify; to appease	
	"The whining child stopped fussing when <u>placated</u> with ice cream."	
	placere to calm; to appease	
placid	**adj.** calm; not easily upset or excited	
	"The Buddha is depicted with a <u>placid</u> expression of inner peace."	
	placere to calm; to appease	
complicit	**adj.** involved with others in an unlawful or devious activity	
	"Co-conspirators were <u>complicit</u> with John Wilkes Booth in Lincoln's assassination."	
	complicare to fold together: *com-* together + *plicare* to fold	
complicity	**n.** the state of being an accomplice	
	"The surprise party required the <u>complicity</u> of her co-workers."	
	comply (v.)	
	complicare to fold together: *com-* together + *plicare* to fold	
duplicity	**n.** deliberate deceptiveness	
	"The wooden horse was a <u>duplicity</u> devised by Odysseus to hoodwink the Trojans."	
	duplex, duplicis twofold; two-faced < *duo* two + *plex, plicis* fold	
implicit	**adj.** implied or understood though not directly expressed; unquestioning and unreserved	
	"Though he voiced no threats, menace was <u>implicit</u> in the villain's tone."	
	imply (v.)	
	implicare to entangle: *im-* in + *plicare* to fold	

Exercise A

Fill in the blanks in the sentences below with the correct form of a word in the scroll above.

1. The Pacific Ocean was named with the superstitious hope that choosing a word representing a _____ place would help to calm the waters.

2. When angered, he became _____ and would brook no suggestion of compromise.

3. The environmental group gathered enough signatures on their _____ to put protection for old-growth forests on the ballot.

4. The child was _____ and well-behaved, making him a favorite with his teenage babysitters.

5. The novice, whose behavior and dress were unconventional, was considered _____ by many of the older nuns.

6. He gave his _____ assent to the deal when he agreed he wouldn't fight the "hostile takeover" bid.

7. Many ancient _____ have been deciphered by archaeologists and linguists.

8. Jack's _____ was enormous; he routinely downed a Whopper, large fries, and a milkshake.

9. The new mayor was not _____ in the bribery and corruption scandal.

10. There was only one other _____ from the United States in the men's figure-skating finals.

11. The elderly widow displayed great _____, attending Mass several times a week and helping at church functions.

12. The rich girl was so used to getting her way that she became _____ whenever her boss suggested ways to improve her performance.

13. Leonardo da Vinci's most famous painting is believed to _____ Monna Lisa del Giocondo.

14. Matt flirted with other women constantly, even after marrying Angela: His _____ was breathtaking.

15. If the school changed divisions, the coach realized that his boys would have to _____ against teams from bigger, wealthier schools.

16. In an attempt to _____ the hungry bear, the campers left the food from their picnic on the ground and beat a quick retreat.

17. Catholics believe that they will _____ their sins if they go to confession.

18. Despite questions about her fitness to serve as vice president, Sarah Palin remained _____ about her ability to tackle even the most complex issues.

19. When the wealthy noble refused to give the beggar a shilling, the impoverished man replied, "it is but a _____."

20. Giving financial assistance to extremist militants is considered _____ in terrorism.

Exercise B

Match the word with the letter of its definition.

1. ___ appetite
2. ___ compete
3. ___ competitor
4. ___ complacent
5. ___ complaisant
6. ___ complicit
7. ___ complicity
8. ___ depict
9. ___ duplicity
10. ___ expiate
11. ___ impious
12. ___ implacable
13. ___ implicit
14. ___ petition
15. ___ petulant
16. ___ pictograph
17. ___ piety
18. ___ pittance
19. ___ placate
20. ___ placid

a) to represent in a picture, sculpture, etc.
b) the state of being an accomplice
c) to make amends for
d) a formal request to an authority
e) irreverent or lacking respect
f) irritable or ill-tempered
g) to strive against another to attain a goal
h) a picture representing a word or idea
i) to calm, pacify, or appease
j) a rival
k) smug and self-satisfied
l) impossible to appease
m) an instinctive physical desire, especially hunger
n) involved with others in an unlawful or shady activity
o) a small amount of money
p) calm
q) deliberate deceptiveness
r) reverence or devotion to a god or gods
s) cheerful and willing to please
t) implied but not readily apparent; unreserved

Exercise C

Solve the crossword puzzle:

Across
1. Inflexible; unwilling to be appeased. 5. To calm, pacify, or appease. 6. Lacking reverence or respect. 8. Deliberate deceptiveness. 11. Calm; not easily upset or excited. 12. A small amount of money. 13. A formal request to a superior authority for a right or benefit. 14. Cheerful and willing to please. 18. The state of being an accomplice.

Down
2. To make amends for. 3. Reverence or devotion to God. 4. A rival. 7. To represent in a picture or sculpture. 9. Smug and self-satisfied. 10. Irritable or ill-tempered. 15. A picture representing a word or idea. 16. Implied or understood, though not directly expressed; unreserved and unquestioning. 17. An instinctive physical desire, especially for food. 18. Involved with others in an unlawful activity. 19. To strive against another to attain a goal or win a contest.

Test 1

Choose the correct meaning for the underlined vocabulary word in each sentence.

1. "There were, in truth, moments when he felt in his turn an impulse, that was nearly resistless, to spring forward and awake the unconscious sleepers; but a glance at Ellen would serve to recall his tottering prudence, and to admonish him of the consequences."

   The Prairie by James Fenimore Cooper

   (a) relieve   (b) warn   (c) relinquish   (d) deceive   (e) inform

2. "But thou art immortal and dost never fade, but bloomest forever in renewed youth."

   Fables by Aesop

   (a) bright   (b) insatiable   (c) sickly   (d) enduring   (e) subject to death

3. "When he rose painfully, the thrusting forward of a skinny groping hand deformed by gouty swellings suggested the effort of a moribund murderer summoning all his remaining strength for a last stab."

   The Secret Agent by Joseph Conrad

   (a) near death   (b) healthy   (c) pathetic   (d) incomplete   (e) wholesome

4. "The paramount importance of these considerations in explaining the immense amount of variation which pigeons have undergone, will be obvious when we treat of selection."

   The Origin of Species by Charles Darwin

   (a) deceptive   (b) questionable   (c) supreme   (d) lacking   (e) perceived

5. "When I had reached these, and walked over the moist, slippery seaweed… to a little mossy promontory with the sea splashing round it, I looked back again to see who next was stirring."

   Agnes Grey by Anne Bronte

   (a) rock   (b) headland   (c) alteration   (d) dormitory   (e) valley

6. "Making a mental note that he would come back some time and study the class of persons that must sit and drink at those multitudinous tables, he proceeded to circumnavigate the room."

The Night-Born by Jack London

   (a) plan a route   (b) enter   (c) tarnish   (d) exit   (e) travel around

7. "The rooms wherein dozens of infants had wailed at their nursing now resounded with the tapping of nascent chicks."

Tess of the d'Urbervilles by Thomas Hardy

   (a) emerging   (b) inborn   (c) native   (d) before birth   (e) naive

8. "Besides, Barbicane's plans would ensure greater perfection for his projectile, and go far to annihilate altogether the effects of the shock."

From The Earth To The Moon by Jules Verne

   (a) recognize   (b) forget   (c) destroy   (d) amplify   (e) change

9. "In the penultimate verse he makes known his discovery concerning the root of modern Nihilism and indifference."

Thus Spake Zarathustra by Friedrich Nietzsche

   (a) hatred   (b) an African religion   (c) prejudice
   (d) denial of morality   (e) elitism

10. "We procured the services of a gentleman experienced in the nomenclature of the American bar, and moved upon the works of one of these impostors."

The Innocents Abroad by Mark Twain

   (a) philosophy   (b) terminology   (c) filing system
   (d) musical notation   (e) numbering

11. "Late hours, nocturnal cigars, and midnight drinkings, pleasurable though they may be, consume too quickly the free-flowing lamps of youth, and are fatal at once to the husbanded candle-ends of age."

Phineas Redux by Anthony Trollope

   (a) musical   (b) aromatic   (c) romantic   (d) poetic   (e) night-time

12. "His renown and his fortune were great enough for M."

The Man in the Iron Mask by Alexandre Dumas

   (a) fame   (b) connections   (c) title   (d) strength   (e) name

13. "Whoever wishes to attain an English style, familiar but not coarse, and elegant but not <u>ostentatious</u>, must give his days and nights to the volumes of Addison."

    Life of Addison by Samuel Johnson

    (a) immodest (b) ornate (c) showy (d) rich (e) decadent

14. "Monsieur Defarge's <u>olfactory</u> sense was by no means delicate, but the stock of wine smelt much stronger than it ever tasted, and so did the stock of rum and brandy and aniseed."

    A Tale Of Two Cities by Charles Dickens

    (a) opening (b) of smell (c) alcoholic (d) of taste (e) ethical

15. To Laius, King of Thebes, an <u>oracle</u> foretold that the child born to him by his queen Jocasta would slay his father and wed his mother."

    Oedipus The King by Sophocles

    (a) sphere (b) politician (c) manuscript (d) prophet (e) speech

16. "The pageant of the wild flowers vanished until all that lingered on the burnt hillsides were orange poppies faded to palest gold, and Mariposa lilies, wind-blown on slender stems amidst the desiccated grasses, that smouldered like <u>ornate</u> spotted moths fluttering in rest for a space between flight and flight."

    Michael, Brother of Jerry by Jack London

    (a) apparently true (b) highly decorated (c) very colorful (d) powdery
    (e) tending to obstruct

17. "Must it not be to that famous elephant, with jeweled tusks, and <u>redolent</u> with myrrh, which was led out of an Indian town to do honor to Alexander the Great?"

    Moby Dick by Herman Melville

    (a) elaborate (b) hateful (c) showy (d) fragrant (e) smelly

18. "Nothing could console and nothing could <u>appease</u> her."

    Pride and Prejudice by Jane Austen

    (a) oppose (b) mitigate (c) save (d) support (e) soothe

19. "In the gray of the morning the two students, <u>pallid</u> and haggard from anxiety and with the terror of their adventure still beating tumultuously in their blood, met at the

medical college."

Can Such Things Be? by Ambrose Bierce

(a) peaceful   (b) gloomy   (c) disguised   (d) pale   (e) darkened

20. "Phileas Fogg, then, had won the twenty thousand pounds; but, as he had spent nearly nineteen thousand on the way, the <u>pecuniary</u> gain was small."

Around The World In Eighty Days by Jules Verne

(a) philosophical   (b) spiritual   (c) financial   (d) physical   (e) exceptional

21. "Lady Susan finds it necessary that Frederica should be to blame, and probably has sometimes judged it <u>expedient</u> to excuse her of ill-nature and sometimes to lament her want of sense."

Lady Susan by Jane Austen

(a) forceful   (b) convenient   (c) unnecessary   (d) delicate   (e) urgent

22. "The growing crowd, he said, was becoming a serious <u>impediment</u> to their excavations, especially the boys."

The War Of The Worlds by H.G. Wells

(a) obstacle   (b) gable   (c) lever   (d) ordinary   (e) genealogy

23. "Sydney Carton looked at his punch and looked at his <u>complacent</u> friend; drank his punch and looked at his <u>complacent</u> friend."

A Tale Of Two Cities by Charles Dickens

(a) obliging   (b) surreptitious   (c) self-satisfied   (d) easily upset   (e) deliberate

24. "She ceased to be a woman, complex, kind and <u>petulant</u>, considerate and thoughtless; she was a Maenad."

Moon and Sixpence by W. Somerset Maugham

(a) formal   (b) physical   (c) ostentatious   (d) peevish   (e) pictorial representation

25. "That is, the capitalists had striven to <u>placate</u> the workers by interesting them financially in their work."

The Iron Heel by Jack London

(a) castigate   (b) represent   (c) atone   (d) deceive   (e) pacify

Lesson VIII
pon/pos/posit, pondero, pons, port/portat

PON, POS, POSIT
to place, to put

PONDERO
weight

PONS
bridge

PORT, PORTAT
to carry

depose, exponent, expose, impose, imposter, interpose, postpone, proponent, superimpose, transpose, imponderable, ponderous, preponderant, pontiff, pontificate, deport, export, import, portable, rapport

Word Definitions

depose
v. to remove from a position of power
"King Charles was <u>deposed</u> by Parliament and later executed."
deposition (n.)
deponere to put down: *de-* down from + *ponere* to put or place

exponent
n. one who supports or interprets; one who represents (something); a mathematical symbol showing the power a number should be raised to
"Eco-friendly citizens are not merely <u>exponents</u> but also practitioners of recycling."
exponential (adj.)
exponere to expound or explain: *ex-* out + *ponere* to put or place

expose
v. to make visible by uncovering
"The investigative reporter <u>exposed</u> corruption in city hall."
exposition (n.)
exponere to expound or explain: *ex-* out + *ponere* to put or place

impose
v. to make mandatory; to force to be accepted, done, or complied with
"The Stamp Act <u>imposed</u> a tax on all publications and printed documents."
imposition (n.)
imponere to inflict; to deceive: *im-* on, upon + *ponere* to put or place

imposter	**n.** a person who deceives by taking a false identity "A wolf in sheep's clothing is a familiar metaphor for an <u>imposter</u>." *imponere* to inflict; to deceive: *im-* on, upon + *ponere* to put or place
interpose	**v.** to insert or introduce between parts; to interject (a remark) "A solar eclipse occurs when the moon <u>interposes</u> between the earth and the sun." *interponere* to put in, introduce: *inter-* between + *ponere* to put or place
postpone	**v.** to put off until a later time "Snow caused the superintendent to <u>postpone</u> the start of school." *postponere* to neglect; to make secondary: *post-* after + *ponere* to put or place
proponent	**n.** an advocate; an open supporter "An atomic power <u>proponent</u>, Admiral Rickover lobbied for the nuclear submarine." *proponere* to propose; to set forth: *pro-* forth + *ponere* to put or place
superimpose	**v.** to place or to lay over another "An inspection renewal sticker is <u>superimposed</u> on the previous year's decal." *superimposition (n.)* *super-* above, beyond + *ponere* to put or place
transpose	**v.** to interchange; to cause to exchange places; to change keys in (music) "He <u>transposed</u> the aria from A minor to D minor to accommodate the mezzo soprano's range." *transposition (n.)* *transponere* to transfer: *trans-* across + *ponere* to put or place
imponderable	**adj.** incapable of being weighed, measured, or thought about "Uncertain weather, unknown currents, and other <u>imponderable</u> factors make a sea voyage risky." *im-* not + *pondus, ponderis* weight; burden
ponderous	**adj.** having great weight; labored and dull "The windy and dull keynoter gave a <u>ponderous</u> speech." *pondus, ponderis* weight
preponderant	**adj.** having superior weight, force, importance, or influence "Protestantism is the <u>preponderant</u> religion in the United States." *pre-* before + *ponderare* to weigh < *pondus, ponderis* weight
pontiff	**n.** the Pope or a bishop "Pope John Paul was the first Polish <u>pontiff</u>." *pontifex* high priest < *pons, pontis* bridge + *facere* to make
pontificate	**n.** the office or term of office of a pontiff **v.** to express one's opinions in a pompous and dogmatic way "Listening to James <u>pontificate</u> on morality filled Jane with loathing."

pontification (n.)
pontifex pontifex < *pons, pontis* bridge + *facere* to make

deport v. to expel from a country
"Foreigners arriving without a passport are immediately deported."
deportation (n.)
deportare to transport; to take home: *de-* away + *portare* to carry

export v. to sells goods and services to another country; to send abroad
n. a good or service sold to other countries; something sent abroad
"Castro tried to export his version of communism to Africa."
exportation (n.)
exportare to export: *ex-* out + *portare* to carry

import v. to bring in (from overseas or another country)
n. a good or service brought in from another country; weight or substance
"His remarks carried no great import, but provided some entertainment."
importation (n.)
importare to bring in: *im-* in + *portare* to carry

portable adj. easily carried or moved
"A picnic can be a portable feast."
portability (n.)
portare to carry

rapport n. a sympathetic relationship; a mutual understanding
"The Stockholm syndrome describes the rapport and dependence hostages feel toward their captors."
apportare to bring toward: *ad-* toward + *portare* to carry

Exercise A

Fill in the blanks in the sentences below with the correct form of a word in the scroll above.

1. Some solar appliances are _____ and can be transported easily to places where they are needed most.

2. He tried to _____ his concerns, but once she began talking, she was like a steamroller.

3. The nature of the universe is largely _____ and unknowable.

4. Angela asked her piano accompanist if he could _____ the song into a higher key so it would fit her voice range better.

5. We must _____ as much as we import to maintain a balance of trade.

6. After the government of Singapore decided to _____ severe punishments for nominal crimes, its crime rate became one of the lowest in the world.

7. When Barbara went to guest services at the casino to claim her $5,000 cash prize, she found that an _____ had beat her to it and fled with her money.

8. In the collage, the artist _____ the faces of renowned politicians on the bodies of pigs, pitbulls, and other animals.

9. During every class, the professor would _____ on his personal opinions of the poets, instead of interpreting their poetry in a historical context.

10. President Bush is an _____ of tax cuts for the wealthiest citizens.

11. Mel Gibson's sword in *Braveheart* appears _____, but he wields it with great skill and agility.

12. Because of torrential rain, the Red Sox had to _____ their game.

13. After a court ruled that his father should have custody of him, Elian Gonzalez was _____ to Cuba over his American relatives' objections.

14. Alfred Stroessner, the dictator of Paraguay for 34 years, was _____ by his second in command, Gen. Andres Rodriguez.

15. The United States depends on the Middle East for much of the oil it _____ .

16. American Catholics had hoped that a new _____ would be less conservative and more in tune with the exigencies of modern life.

17. We removed layers of wallpaper to _____ the original walls.

18. The _____ language spoken by the Mayans of northern Guatemala is Quiche, although there are many local dialects.

19. The sheriff was a strong _____ of making handguns illegal.

20. A _____ built on mutual trust and understanding is a solid base for a successful marriage.

Exercise B

Match the word with the letter of its definition.

1. ___ deport
2. ___ depose
3. ___ exponent
4. ___ export
5. ___ expose
6. ___ imponderable
7. ___ import
8. ___ impose
9. ___ imposter
10. ___ interpose
11. ___ ponderous
12. ___ pontiff
13. ___ pontificate
14. ___ portable
15. ___ postpone
16. ___ preponderant
17. ___ proponent
18. ___ rapport
19. ___ superimpose
20. ___ transpose

a) having great weight
b) the Pope or a bishop
c) to insert or introduce between parts; to interject
d) incapable of being weighed, measured, or thought about
e) easily carried or moved
f) to make visible by uncovering
g) to hold forth pompously on one's opinions
h) one who supports or represents (a cause)
i) to put off until a later time
j) having superior weight, force, or importance
k) an advocate
l) to remove from a position of power
m) to bring in (from overseas)
n) to place or lay over something else
o) to send to another country for sale
p) to require (by force or by law)
q) a sympathetic relationship
r) to interchange
s) to expel from a country
t) a person who deceives by taking a false identity

Exercise C

Across
4. To make something mandatory; to force to be accepted, done, or compiled with. 7. Having great weight. 8. To interchange; to cause to exchange places; to change keys (in music). 9. Having superior weight, force, importance, or influence. 11. Incapable of being weighed or measured. 15. One who supports or represents; one who expounds or interprets. 16. A person who deceives by taking a false identity. 17. The office or term of office of a pontiff.

Down
1. To place or lay on top of something else. 2. Easily carried or moved. 3. To expel from a country. 4. To bring in. 5. An advocate or supporter. 6. To remove from a position of power. 9. The Pope or a bishop. 10. A mutual understanding. 11. To insert or introduce between parts; to interject (a remark). 12. To put off until a later time. 13. To make visible by uncovering. 14. To sell goods and services to another country.

Lesson IX

portus, pot/poten, pota-, praeda, prehend-, press-

PORTUS
harbor, port

POTEN-
able, powerful

POTA-
to drink

PRAEDA
plunder, loot

PREHEND-
to catch, to grasp

PRESSUS
pressed

*opportune, opportunist, impotent, potentate, potential, puissant,
potable, potion, depredate, predatory, apprehend, comprise,
reprehend, reprisal, compress, depressed, express, impress, oppress*

Word Definitions

opportune
adj. suited or right for a particular purpose; especially convenient or appropriate
"Mistletoe provides an opportune excuse to plant a kiss."
opportunity (n.)
opportunus suitable; favorable < *ob-* toward + *portum* port < *portus* harbor; refuge

opportunist
n. a person who takes advantage of any chance to achieve an end
"An opportunist, he bought houses from desperate homeowners for much less than their assessed."
opportunus suitable; favorable < *ob-* toward + *portum* port < *portus* harbor; refuge

impotent
adj. weak; helpless; powerless
"Samson was rendered impotent when Delilah cut off his hair."
impotence (n.)
im- not + *potens, potentis* powerful; strong < *posse* to be powerful; to be able

potentate
n. a monarch
"The potentate of the Mongols was their leader, Genghis Khan."
potens, potentis powerful; strong < *posse* to be powerful; to be able

potential   **adj.** the capacity for future development
"The scandal had the potential to derail his candidacy."
potentia power; force < *posse* to be powerful; to be able

puissant   **adj.** having great power or influence
"The puissant ant is capable of carrying 50 times its own weight."
posse to be powerful or strong

potable   **adj.** drinkable
"Desalinization plants can make seawater potable."
potare to drink

potion   **n.** a liquid with healing, magical, or poisonous properties; a liquid concoction
"Absinthe liqueur contains wood alcohol, making it a poisonous potion."
potare to drink

depredate   **v.** to plunder or ravage
"A wrinkled face, a halting gait, and failing eyesight are depredations of old age."
depredation (n.)
de- completely + *praedare* to plunder < *praeda* loot, booty; prey

predatory   **adj.** characterized by plundering; preying on others
"Loan sharks charge such predatory interest rates that their dealings are illegal."
predator (n.)
praedatus (past participle of the verb *praedare* to plunder)

apprehend   **v.** to take into custody for a crime; to perceive; to understand
"Robert E. Lee apprehended John Brown in the Harper's Ferry armory."
apprehension (n.)
apprehendere to seize upon; to overtake: *ad-* toward + *prehendere* to grasp; to capture

comprise   **v.** to consist of; to include or contain; to form or constitute
"A Roman legion comprised 3,000 to 6,000 foot soldiers and 100 to 200 cavalry troops."
comprehendere to grasp firmly; to deal with: *com-* together + *prehendere* to grasp; to capture

reprehend   **v.** to censure; to reprimand; to rebuke
"The teenager was reprehended and grounded for driving without permission."
reprehension (n.)
reprehendere to seize; to blame: *re-* again (expressing intensity) + *prehendere* to grasp; to capture

reprisal   **n.** an act of retaliation
"A trade embargo was the U.S. reprisal for Castro's politics."
reprehendere to seize; to blame: *re-* again + *prehendere* to grasp; to capture

compress	**v.** to make more compact by pressing together "A digest <u>compresses</u> a book or article into a shortened or summarized version." *compression (n.)* *compressus* compression; pressure: *com-* together + *pressus* pressed (past participle of the verb *premere* to press)
depressed	**adj.** dejected in spirit or position "Capital letters are formed on the keyboard by <u>depressing</u> the shift and letter keys simultaneously." *depression (n.), depress (v.)* *depressus* pressed down; depressed: *de-* down + *pressus* pressed
express	**v.** to state; to convey by words, gestures, conduct, or facial expression "The soldier <u>expressed</u> his gratitude to the medics who pulled him from the battlefield." *expression (n.)* *expressus* distinct; visible: *ex-* out + *pressus* pressed
impress	**v.** to affect strongly (especially favorably) "The doctor <u>impressed</u> the patient with the importance of regular exercise." *impression (n.)* *impressus* imprinted; stamped; impressed: *im-* into + *pressus* pressed
oppress	**v.** to keep down by unjust authority "Slaves were <u>oppressed</u> by demanding masters and backbreaking work." *oppression (n.)* *oppressus* to crush; to press against: *ob-* against, over + *pressus* pressed

Exercise A

Fill in the blanks in the sentences below with the correct form of a word in the scroll above.

1. When the mother scolded her daughter, she did not expect a violent _____ , but her daughter surprised her by pushing her down.

2. If you wish me to understand what you are saying, please stop mumbling and _____ yourself coherently.

3. The real estate broker highlighted the house's convenient location when showing it to _____ buyers.

4. Michael Jordan tries to _____ upon young athletes the importance of staying away from drugs and alcohol.

5. Some campgrounds have signs over their restroom sinks that say "not _____," meaning the water is for washing but not for drinking.

6. The Aerobed, once deflated, can be _____ into a small sack for easy storage or travel.

7. After successfully concluding a major project, Jim decided it was an _____ time to ask his boss for a raise.

8. She tried not to get _____ when her favorite cat died.

9. England, once a _____ nation with a far-reaching empire, has seen its power and influence contract since World War II.

10. He raged at the witness, but his manacles and ankle shackles ensured he was _____ to harm her.

11. The _____ pirates trolled the coast of Somalia, trying to capture merchant ships.

12. Every time she tried to voice an opinion, Bill O'Reilly _____ her with sarcastic interruptions and attacks.

13. King Charles I of England was an infamous _____ who attempted to take power away from Parliament, but failed.

14. The herbalist combined several ingredients, then asked the patient to drink the _____.

15. Six countries _____ the original European Union, which has now grown into an economic power capable of competing with the United States.

16. Everyone saw him as an _____ because he took advantage of vulnerable people, especially elderly widows with little financial expertise.

17. The lawyer _____ her client for talking with the reporters.

18. The infamous pirate Blackbeard sailed among the coastal towns of North and South Carolina to _____ the settlers.

19. Some of the police who _____ him later came to believe he was innocent of the murder, and testified as defense witnesses on retrial.

Exercise B

Match the word with the letter of its definition.

1. ___ apprehend
2. ___ compress
3. ___ comprise
4. ___ depredate
5. ___ depressed
6. ___ express
7. ___ impotent
8. ___ impress
9. ___ opportune
10. ___ opportunist
11. ___ oppress
12. ___ potable
13. ___ potentate
14. ___ potential
15. ___ potion
16. ___ predatory
17. ___ puissant
18. ___ reprehend
19. ___ reprisal

a) a monarch
b) to reprimand or rebuke
c) preying on others
d) to affect strongly (especially favorably)
e) to plunder; to ravage
f) having the capacity for development
g) an act of retaliation
h) very convenient or appropriate
i) to consist of
j) to arrest for a crime
k) having great power or influence
l) helpless or powerless
m) drinkable
n) to keep down by unjust authority
o) to make more compact by pressing
p) a liquid or liquid mixture with medical or magical properties
q) dejected in spirit or position
r) to communicate (something)
s) a person who takes advantage of any opportunity to achieve an end

Exercise C

Solve the crossword puzzle.

Across
1 Characterized by plundering; preying on others 8 To consist of 9 Suited or right for a particular purpose 12 Dejected in spirit or position 16 Weak; helpless; powerless 17 An act of retaliation 18 To state; to convey by words, gestures, conduct 19 A liquid with healing, magical, or poisonous properties

Down
2 To censure; to reprimand; to rebuke 3 To take into custody for a crime 4 A person who takes advantage of any chance to achieve an end 5 To plunder or ravage 6 A monarch 7 To keep down by unjust authority 10 The capacity for future development 11 To make more compact by pressing together 13 Having great power or influence 14 To affect strongly (especially favorably) 15 Drinkable

Lesson X

prob-, puer, pugn-, pung-/punc-, puni-, puta-

PROB-
to test

PUER
child, boy

PUGN-
to fight

PUNG-/PUNC-
to puncture

PUNI-
to punish

PUTA-
to trim, calculate, consider, think

approbation, reprobate, reprove, puerile, impugn, pugilism, pugnacious, compunction, expunge, punctilious, pungent, impunity, punish, punitive, amputate, compute, computer, putative, reputation, reputed

Word Definitions

approbation
n. praise; warm approval for an achievement
"Lengthy applause and shouts of approbation greeted the returning hero."
approbate (v.)
approbare to approve: *ad-* to + *probare* to try; to examine

reprobate
n. an unprincipled person
"Reprobates are condemned to damnation for their moral bankruptcy."
reprobation (n.)
reprobare to condemn or reject: *re-* back (expressing negation) + *probare* to try; to examine; to test or probe

reprove
v. to voice or convey disapproval of; to rebuke or reprimand
"English schoolmasters reproved misbehaving boys by caning them."
reprobare to condemn or reject: *re-* back (expressing negation) + *probare* to try; to examine; to test or probe

puerile
adj. childish
"Even adults like occasional puerile pursuits such as water fights and playground slides."
puer child (boy); servant

impugn
v. to attack; to dispute the truth, validity, or honesty of
"To challenge the truth of his testimony is to impugn the witness."
impugnare to assail: *im-* against + *pugnare* to fight

pugilism
n. the sport of boxing
"Olympic boxers of Ancient Greece engaged in pugilism without gloves."
pugilatus boxing < *pugnare* to fight

pugnacious	**adj.** belligerent; eager or quick to argue, quarrel, or fight "Often itching for a fight, bullies exhibit <u>pugnacious</u> behavior." *pugnax, pugnacis* pugnacious < *pugnare* to fight
compunction	**n.** a sting of conscience or a pang of doubt aroused by wrongdoing "He felt no <u>compunction</u> about not tipping the obnoxious waiter." *com-* with + *pungere* to prick or puncture
expunge	**v.** to erase or strike out "Juvenile arrest records are usually <u>expunged</u> when the offender reaches adulthood." *ex-* out + *pungere* to prick or puncture; to mark with points or pricks
punctilious	**adj.** strictly attentive to minute details of form in action or conduct; precise "A good auditor is <u>punctilious</u> in reviewing client tax returns." *punctus* marked with points (past participle of the verb *pungere* to prick)
pungent	**adj.** biting or caustic; describing a very strong taste or smell "'A Modest Proposal' was Swift's <u>pungent</u> satire of English attitudes toward Ireland." *pungere* to prick or puncture
impunity	**n.** exemption from punishment "Not subject to local laws, diplomats often commit minor crimes with <u>impunity</u>." *im-* not + *poena* penalty; retribution
punish	**v.** to inflict a penalty on (someone) for an offense "Psychologists claim that to <u>punish</u> children by spanking is to invite more aggressive behavior." *punishment (n.)* *punire* to punish; to avenge < *poena* penalty; retribution
punitive	**adj.** inflicting pain or aiming to inflict punishment "While a fine is a <u>punitive</u> payment, a tax is a citizen's duty." *punitus* punished (past participle of the verb *punire* to punish; to avenge) <
amputate	**v.** to cut off (especially a part of the body) "The onset of gangrene in his leg required <u>amputation</u> below the knee." *amputation (n.)* *amputare* to cut off; to prune: *am-, ambi-* around + *putare* to trim; to calculate, consider, or think
compute	**v.** to determine by mathematics; to determine by arithmetic or mathematical reasoning "One <u>computes</u> on an abacus by pushing beads along wires stretched in a rigid frame." *computation (n.)* *computare* to calculate: *com-* together + *putare* to think; to estimate or value

computer   **n.** a device that computes
"Charles Babbage's *Difference Engine* was the first programmable computer."
computare to calculate: *com-* together + *putare* to think; to estimate or value

putative   **adj.** generally regarded as such; supposed
"The father is the putative head-of-household, but the mother really runs the show."
putare to think; to estimate or value

reputation   **n.** a general opinion of someone's character; the beliefs or opinions generally held about someone or something
"She gained a reputation as a thoughtful, incisive political commentator."
reputare to think over; to reflect: *re-* again + *putare* to think

reputed   **adj.** having a reputation (for something)
"Although reputed to be a pirate, Captain Kidd was probably a government agent."
reputare to think over; to reflect: *re-* again + *putare* to think

Exercise A

Fill in the blanks in the sentences below with the correct form of a word in the scroll above.

1. He was most _____ in dress and manner, but not so precise in his work.

2. Mike Tyson's style of _____ has harmed the reputation of boxing.

3. The job required him to _____ receipts and expenses daily.

4. To _____ offenders for speeding, officers hand out tickets requiring them to pay fines.

5. After more than a year, his patent met with _____ from the patent bureau.

6. The chef at L'Espalier was _____ to be the best in Boston.

7. The presidential candidates _____ each others' reputations.

8. The unhappy, _____ man was always picking arguments with co-workers, clerks, and neighbors – really almost everyone he encountered.

9. The young stockbroker's leisure hours were spent in _____ pursuits such as reading comic books and playing computer fantasy games.

10. Editors at *The Boston Globe* try to _____ errors from articles before they are published, but a few still make it into print.

11. Often mathematicians require the assistance of a _____ for complex calculations.

12. His _____ reason for visiting the museum was to see the special photography exhibit, but actually he was hoping to run into Miranda.

13. He was an old _____, and his son was no better; he adopted his father's habits of making sleazy deals and bribing officials to look the other way.

14. Her intent in sentencing the homeless drunk to jail was _____, but he expressed relief at having a place to stay and three meals a day.

15. The abandoned house was filled with the _____ odor of rotten eggs.

16. The ruthless bully felt no _____ after beating up the little boy on the playground and stealing his lunch money.

17. The soldier's life was spared, even though the surgeon was forced to _____ parts of both legs.

18. No matter how many times the teacher _____ the mischievous boy, he continued his antics because they made him popular with the other children.

19. Her _____ preceded her, and everyone at her new company welcomed her firm, but pleasant, style of leadership.

20. Although he was the driver of the getaway car, Darius received _____ in exchange for his testimony against the gunman.

Exercise B

Match the word with the letter of its definition.

1. ___ amputate
2. ___ approbation
3. ___ compunction
4. ___ compute
5. ___ computer
6. ___ expunge
7. ___ impugn
8. ___ impunity
9. ___ puerile
10. ___ pugilism
11. ___ pugnacious
12. ___ punctilious
13. ___ pungent
14. ___ punish
15. ___ punitive
16. ___ putative
17. ___ reprobate
18. ___ reprove
19. ___ reputation
20. ___ reputed

a) exemption from punishment
b) to rebuke or reprimand
c) inflicting or intended as punishment
d) to determine by mathematics
e) eager or quick to argue, quarrel, or fight
f) biting or caustic
g) to cut off a part of the body
h) an unprincipled person
i) generally regarded as such; supposed
j) to erase or strike out
k) childish
l) having a reputation as
m) a device that computes
n) to inflict a penalty as retribution
o) strictly attentive to minute details
p) praise; an expression of warm approval
q) to dispute the truth, validity, or honesty of
r) the sport of boxing
s) a pang of doubt aroused by wrongdoing
t) a general opinion of someone's character

Exercise C

Solve the crossword puzzle:

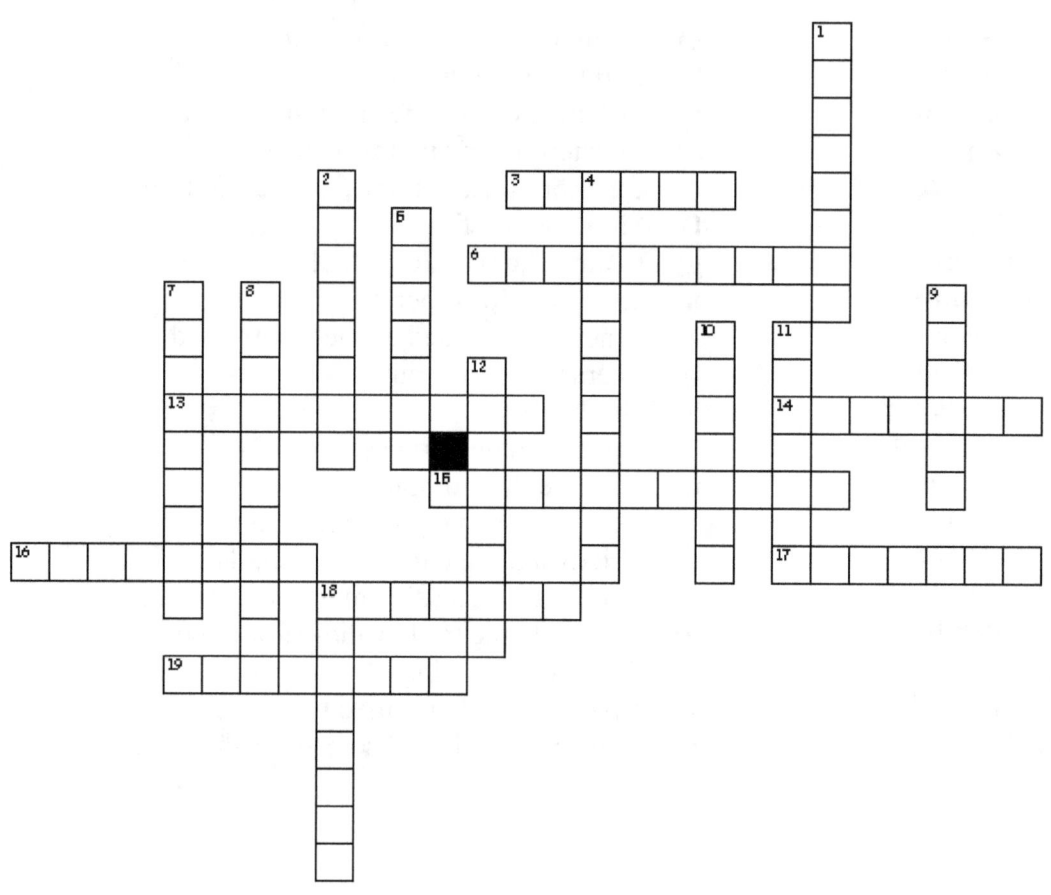

Across
3. To attack; to dispute the truth, validity, or honesty of. 6. Belligerent; eager or quick to argue, quarrel, or fight. 13. The beliefs or opinions generally held about someone or something. 14. Childish. 15. An expression of warm approval for an accomplishment. 16. To cut off (especially a part of the body). 17. To erase or strike out. 18. Biting or caustic. 19. Inflicting pain or aiming to inflict punishment.

Down
1. The sport of boxing. 2. Exemption from punishment. 4. Strictly attentive to minute details in action or conduct; precise. 5. To determine by mathematics. 7. An unprincipled person. 8. A sting of conscience or a pang of doubt aroused by wrongdoing. 9. To inflict a penalty on (someone) as retribution for an offense. 10. Having a reputation (as something). 11. To voice or convey disapproval of; to rebuke or reprimand. 12. A device that computes. 18. Generally regarded as such; supposed.

Lesson XI
rap-, ratio, reg-/rect-/regent, rid-/ris-

RAP-
to snatch, seize

RATIO
reasoning, rule

REG-, RECT-, REGENT
to rule, to guide, to govern

RID-, RIS-
to laugh

---

rapacious, rapture, ravish, arraign, ratio, rational, rationale, rationalize, directive, incorrigible, insurgent, insurrection, rectify, regular, regent rector, deride, ridicule, ridiculous, risible

---

Word Definitions

rapacious **adj.** aggressively greedy
"The Vikings were <u>rapacious</u> raiders who pillaged, plundered, and burned villages."
rapere to seize; to destroy

rapture **n.** a feeling of intense pleasure or joy
"When first given news of the award, a Nobel Prize winner probably feels complete <u>rapture</u>."
rapere to seize; to destroy

ravish **v.** to fill with intense delight; to seize or carry off by force; to rape
"Taking the form of a swan, Zeus <u>ravished</u> the maiden Leda to beget Helen."
rapere to seize; to destroy

arraign **v.** to call before a court to face charges
"When a defendant is <u>arraigned</u>, he or she may be required to enter a plea."
arraignment (n.)
ad- to + *ratio* reckoning or account; reasoning; rule

ratio **n.** the quantitative relation between two amounts showing the number of times one value contains or is contained within the other
"The Golden <u>Ratio</u>, or Φ (roughly 1.6 to 1), underlies the graceful

proportions of Greek architecture."
ratio account; reasoning; rule (in mathematics)

rational   **adj.** based on or in accordance with reason or logic
"To an economist, rational action may be either 'sensible,' 'efficient,' or both."
rationality (n.)
ratio account; reasoning; rule < *reri* to reason; to reckon

rationale   **n.** a set of reasons or a logical basis for a course of action or a belief; an excuse
"The rationale for building the Panama Canal was economy of time and money in shipping."
ratio account; reasoning; rule < *reri* to reason; to reckon

rationalize   **v.** to attempt to justify with logical reasoning; to devise self-satisfying but false reasons for one's behavior or feelings
"Aesop's fox, unable to reach the grapes, rationalized that they were probably sour."
ratio account; reasoning; rule < *reri* to reason; to reckon

directive   **n.** an official or authoritative instruction
adj. involving the direction of operations
"President Kennedy issued a directive to the navy to blockade Cuba in October 1962."
dirigere to direct; to set in order: *di-* down + *rigere* to stand straight or be rigid

incorrigible   **adj.** not able to be corrected or reformed
"An incorrigible liar is incapable of ever learning or being persuaded to tell the truth."
in- not + *corrigere* to correct: *co-* together + *rigere* to stand straight or be rigid

insurgent   **n.** a rebel or revolutionary
"Initially a leader of the insurgent fighters who overthrew the corrupt dictator Batista, Fidel Castro went on to become a dictator himself."
insurgere to rise up against: *in-* against + *surgere* to rise up; to grow

insurrection   **n.** a violent uprising against authority
"A mutiny is an insurrection or uprising to take control of a ship."
insurgere to rise up against: *in-* against + *surgere* to rise up; to grow

rectify   **v.** to put right; to correct
"The situation was a lost cause and therefore impossible to rectify."
rectificare to rectify; to control < *rectus* right; proper

regular   **adj.** arranged in a consistent or definite pattern; recurring at short intervals; conforming to or governed by an accepted standard of procedure or convention
"The Redcoats were regular soldiers, while the colonials were an irregular

	citizen militia." *regula* rule; standard
regent	**n.** a person appointed to administer a state because the monarch is a minor, or is absent or incapacitated "As regent, Hatshepsut ruled for her young son, Thutmose, whom she soon usurped, becoming the longest-reigning female pharoah." *regere* to rule
rector	**n.** a priest or member of the clergy in charge of a church "A rector, or leader of a church or parish, lives in a rectory." *rector* ruler < *regere* to rule; to guide
deride	**v.** to express contempt for; to ridicule; to scorn "Unappreciated Elizabethan actors were derided with boo's or were hurled rotten vegetables." *deridere* to mock; to scoff at: *de-* down, from + *ridere* to laugh
ridicule	**n.** mockery or derision **v.** subject to mockery "Puritan transgressor had their feet locked in wooden stocks in the town square, where they were subjected to public ridicule." *ridere* to laugh
ridiculous	**adj.** inviting ridicule; absurd "Political cartoons often exaggerate facial features to make politicians look ridiculous." *ridere* to laugh
risible	**adj.** such as to provoke laughter "The clowns amused the crowd with risible antics." *risus* laughter

Exercise A

Fill in the blanks in the sentences below with the correct form of a word in the scroll above.

1. The delinquent teenager seemed _____ , so his parents sent him to a military academy, hoping the strict discipline would improve his behavior.

2. Some children have a tendency to _____ others whom they see as different, especially other kids who dress badly or are overweight.

3. The corporation issued a _____ to all division heads, requiring them to cut their expenses by 10 percent.

4. Percentages and _____ are among the standard mathematical concepts tested on college admissions exams.

5. When Edward, the son of Henry VIII and Jane Seymour, became king, his _____ was a maternal uncle.

6. The view of the sun setting behind the distant hills added to their romantic feelings of _____.

7. The carpenter tried to _____ the defects in his construction by blaming them on the lumber the client had ordered.

8. Don't kid yourself that he's doing you a favor: He's the most cutthroat and _____ stockbroker I know.

9. The _____ were quickly surrounded by the army.

10. The _____ graciously greeted the members of the congregation as they left the sanctuary.

11. She _____ him for his low salary, his timidity, and his rough manners.

12. The judge waited to _____ the suspect until his lawyer arrived.

13. The American Revolution started as an _____ against the British rulers.

14. A _____ polygon is one whose sides are all of equal length.

15. The groom and his attendants wore kilts to the wedding, which to a few guests looked _____.

16. When the college student angrily kicked in the door of his dorm room, he used the fact that his roommate had locked him out as a _____ for his destructive act.

17. She _____ him with her beauty and intelligence.

18. The director attempted to _____ the actor's awkward delivery by having him do a voice-over.

19. The girl's slip on a banana peel might not have been enjoyable for her, but presented a _____ sight for everyone watching.

20. If you could just explain your concern in a _____ way instead of yelling, you might be more successful in convincing me to let you have your way.

Exercise B

Match the word with the letter of its definition.

1. ___ arraign
2. ___ deride
3. ___ directive
4. ___ incorrigible
5. ___ insurgent
6. ___ insurrection
7. ___ rapacious
8. ___ rapture
9. ___ ratio
10. ___ rational
11. ___ rationale
12. ___ rationalize
13. ___ ravish
14. ___ rectify
15. ___ regular
16. ___ regent
17. ___ rector
18. ___ ridicule
19. ___ ridiculous
20. ___ risible

a) an uprising against authority
b) a member of the clergy in charge of a church
c) a logical basis for an action or belief; an excuse
d) to bring before a court to face charges
e) mockery or derision
f) an official or authoritative instruction
g) such as to provoke laughter
h) to put right; to correct
i) a rebel or revolutionary
j) inviting ridicule; absurd
k) aggressively greedy
l) to scoff at; to mock
m) to attempt to justify with logical reasoning
n) arranged in a consistent or definite pattern
o) unable to be corrected or reformed
p) based on or in accordance with reason or logic
q) to fill with intense delight; to seize by force
r) a feeling of intense pleasure or joy
s) the quantitative relation between two amounts
t) a person appointed to administer a state because the monarch is a minor or is absent

Exercise C

Solve the crossword puzzle.

Across
1. The quantitative relation between two amounts showing the proportion of one to the other. 4. To bring before a court to face charges. 6. A rebel or revolutionary. 8. Inviting ridicule; absurd. 12. Not able to be corrected or reformed. 14. A set of reasons or a logical basis for a course of action or a belief; an excuse. 15. Mockery or derision. 16. An official or authoritative instruction. 17. A person appointed to govern a state because the monarch is a minor, or is absent or incapacitated. 18. To attempt to justify with logical reasoning.

Down
1. Aggressively greedy. 2. Such as to provoke laughter. 3. To scoff at; to mock. 5. A priest or member of the clergy in charge of a church. 7. A feeling of intense pleasure or joy. 8. To fill with intense delight; to seize or carry off by force. 9. Arranged in a consistent or definite pattern; recurring at short intervals; conforming to or governed by an accepted standard of procedure or convention. 10. Based on or in accordance with reason or logic. 11. To put right; to correct. 13. A violent uprising against authority.

Lesson XII
rog-/rogat, rota, rupt-, rus

ROG-, ROGAT
to ask, to beg

ROTA
wheel

RUPT-
to break

RUS
country

abrogate, arrogant, arrogate, derogatory, interrogate, interrogative, prerogative, rogue, rotary, rotate, rote, rotund, rotunda abrupt, disrupt, erupt, interrupt, rupture, rustic, rusticate

Word Definitions

abrogate
v. to repeal or to cancel a law or agreement; to violate (a treaty or duty)
"The amendment to repeal Prohibition <u>abrogated</u> a prior amendment that instated it."
abrogation (n.)
abrogare to repeal: *ab-* away + *rogare* to ask for or introduce (a law)

arrogant
adj. having an exaggerated sense of one's own importance or abilities
"The United States, seen by many as an overly proud and boastful power, is viewed by many as <u>arrogant</u>."
arrogance (n.)
arrogare to claim for oneself: *ad-* to + *rogare* to ask for

arrogate
v. to take or claim for oneself without justification
"Since World War II, presidents have <u>arrogated</u> from Congress the right to make war."
arrogare to claim for oneself: *ad-* toward + *rogare* to ask for

derogatory
adj. showing a critical or disrespectful attitude toward; disparaging
"A gourmet would likely make <u>derogatory</u> remarks about the quality of fast food."
derogare to disparage; to set aside: *de-* down, from + *rogare* to ask for

interrogate
v. to ask questions aggressively
"The Inquisition was notorious for <u>interrogating</u> prisoners on pain of torture."

	interrogation (n.) *interrogare* to question; to examine: *inter-* between + *rogare* to ask
interrogative	**adj.** having the force of a question; a question "The <u>interrogative</u> arch of his eyebrows showed his disbelief." *interrogare* to question; to examine: *inter-* between + *rogare* to ask
prerogative	**n.** a right or privilege exclusive to a particular individual or class "A key to the executive washroom is a <u>prerogative</u> of company officers." *pre-* before + *rogare* to ask
rogue	**n.** a dishonest or unprincipled person; a rascal (esp. a child); a person operating out of control; an elephant or other large animal on a rampage "In 'Apocalypse Now,' Kurtz is a <u>rogue</u> American officer with a private native army." *rogare* to ask for or beg
rotary	**adj.** revolving around a center or axis **n.** a traffic circle "The traffic circle Americans call a <u>rotary</u> is what the British call a roundabout." *rotare* to revolve or rotate < *rota* wheel
rotate	**v.** to move in a circle around an axis; to change regularly by turns "Military units are regularly <u>rotated</u> into and out of the war zone." *rotation (n.)* *rotare* to revolve or rotate < *rota* wheel
rote	**adj.** mechanical; routine; learned by memorization "Memorization, or <u>rote</u> learning, is practiced far more in Asian than American schools." *rota* wheel
rotund	**adj.** plump; rounded "Santa Claus is pictured as a well-fed, <u>rotund</u> figure." *rotunda, rotundus* round
rotunda	**n.** a round building or room, especially with a dome "The president's body lies in state beneath the Capitol <u>Rotunda</u>." *rotunda, rotundus* round
abrupt	**adj.** sudden and unexpected; brief to the point of rudeness; curt "He glanced at his watch, stood quickly, and <u>abruptly</u> left the table." *abruptus* hasty; broken < *rumpere* to break off: *ab-* away, from + *rumpere* to break
disrupt	**v.** to disturb or interrupt; to seriously alter or destroy the structure of "Police used water cannon and tear gas to <u>disrupt</u> the protestors' march." *disruption (n.)* *disruptus* broken off (past participle of the verb *disrumpere*, to cause to break apart: *dis-* down from + *rumpere* to break)

erupt	**v.** to forcefully eject lava, rocks, ash, or gases from a volcano; to break out suddenly; to give vent to feelings *eruption (n.)* "The audience <u>erupted</u> in hisses each time the villain appeared." *eruptus* broken out (past participle of the verb *erumpere* to break out: *ex-* out + *rumpere* to break)
interrupt	**v.** to break into the middle of (especially another's speech) "Morse code was sent by <u>interrupted</u> pulses of electricity through telegraph wires." *interruption (n.)* *interruptus* interrupted (past participle of the verb *interrumpere* to break up: *inter-* between + *rumpere* to break)
rupture	**v.** to break or burst suddenly; to breach or to disturb **n.** an instance of bursting; a break or breach "Spherical bombs bouncing off the water's surface hit and <u>ruptured</u> the Ruhr dams." *ruptus* broken; destroyed (past participle of the verb *rumpere* to break)
rustic	**adj.** of or characteristic of life in the country; made of rough materials; primitive or unsophisticated **n.** an unsophisticated country person "Abandoning city life, the utopians took up <u>rustic</u> lives as farmers and herdsmen." *rusticus* rural; plain; homely < *rus* the country; a farm
rusticate	**v.** to go to live in or spend time in the country "Boston Brahmins spent family summers <u>rusticating</u> in Nantucket." *rustication (n.)* *rusticari* to live in the country < *rus* the country; a farm

Exercise A

Fill in the blanks in the sentences below with the correct form of a word in the scroll above.

1. During the turn of the twentieth century, the gentry sought cleaner and purer summer air for their families and escaped city life to _____ near the shore.

2. Insecure people often make _____ remarks about others to make themselves feel superior.

3. Anti-communist demonstrators in the audience _____ the performance by the Russian national ballet.

4. His _____ look made her realize she'd have a lot of explaining to do once the guests had left.

5. He was short and fat, of a _____ shape; he reminded her of a Styrofoam Christmas ball she had decorated as a Santa Claus.

6. Hitler _____ every nonaggression treaty he signed with other European leaders; he used the treaties to deceive them about his intentions until his forces were ready to invade.

7. Even though teachers may claim that late arrivals _____ the class, there probably are more serious disruptions.

8. Orwell's best-known essay examines the cultural forces that drove him to shoot a _____ elephant when he served as a colonial officer in India.

9. *Field of Dreams* showed baseball's _____ roots, with its images of farm boys hitting balls into cornfields.

10. The use of a _____ to keep traffic flowing at busy intersections is an old concept in England, but relatively new in France.

11. It's not a good idea to _____ the right to make decisions for your parents, just because they're getting a little forgetful: They will resent you for it.

12. The children rehearsed their poems so that when it came time to recite them they knew them by _____.

13. Sir Christopher Wren designed St. Paul's Cathedral in London with a magnificent _____.

14. The police began to _____ the suspect about the crime.

15. It is recommended to _____ your tires every 5,000 miles.

16. Larry King is considered by some TV viewers to be _____, because of his self-important attitude when interviewing his guests.

17. The horse looked confident as he approached the jump, but his _____ stop sent the jockey rider sliding over his neck in a sickening fall.

18. Nearby residents evacuated the area, as authorities expected the volcano to _____ within days.

19. I think he wants to become governor more for the _____ and perquisites that come with office than out of a desire to serve the public.

20. A bruise that you get after bumping into something is actually blood from a _____ blood vessel.

Exercise B

Match the word with the letter of its definition.

1. ___ abrogate
2. ___ abrupt
3. ___ arrogant
4. ___ arrogate
5. ___ derogatory
6. ___ disrupt
7. ___ erupt
8. ___ interrogate
9. ___ interrogative
10. ___ interrupt
11. ___ prerogative
12. ___ rogue
13. ___ rotary
14. ___ rotate
15. ___ rote
16. ___ rotund
17. ___ rotunda
18. ___ rupture
19. ___ rustic
20. ___ rusticate

a) to forcefully eject; to break out suddenly
b) mechanical or routine; learned through memorization
c) characteristic of life in the country
d) to move in a circle around an axis
e) sudden and unexpected
f) revolving around a center or axis; a traffic circle
g) a round building, especially with a dome
h) to disturb or interrupt
i) large and plump; rounded
j) to break or burst suddenly
k) having the force of a question; questioning
l) to go live or spend time in the country
m) to repeal or cancel an agreement; to violate a treaty
n) a dishonest or unprincipled man
o) to break into the middle of (something)
p) critical, disrespectful, or disparaging
q) to ask questions aggressively
r) having an exaggerated sense of one's own importance or abilities
s) to claim for oneself without justification
t) a right or privilege exclusive to a particular individual or class

Exercise C

Solve the crossword puzzle.

Across
5. To ask questions aggressively. 7. Revolving around a center or axis; a traffic circle. 8. A round building or room, especially with a dome. 9. Sudden and unexpected; brief to the point of rudeness; curt. 13. To forcefully eject lava, rocks, ash, or gases of a volcano; to break out suddenly; to give vent to feelings. 14. A dishonest or unprincipled man; an elephant or other large animal on a rampage. 16. Critical, disrespectful, or disparaging. 18. Of or characteristic of life in the country; primitive or unsophisticated. 19. To break into the middle of.

Down
1. To go live or spend time in the country. 2. Mechanical or routine; learned through memorization. 3. To disturb or interrupt; to seriously alter or destroy. 4. Having an exaggerated sense of one's own importance or abilities. 6. To take or claim for oneself without justification. 8. To move in a circle around an axis. 10. To break or burst suddenly; to breach or disturb. 11. Having the force of a question; questioning. 12. A right or privilege exclusive to a particular individual or class. 15. Plump. 17. To repeal or cancel a law or agreement; to violate (a treaty or duty).

Lesson XIII
sacr-/sanctus, sagac-, sapere, salire/sult-, salis, sanguis

SACR-, SANCTUS
holy

SAGAC-, SAPERE
to perceive, to know

SALIRE, SULT-
to leap

SALIS
salt

SANGUIS
blood, family

consecrate, execrate, sacrament, sacred, sacrilege, sanctify, sanctimonious, sanction, sanctity, sanctum, presage, sagacious, sapient, assail, assault, exult, insult, saline, consanguinity, sanguine

Word Definitions

consecrate v. to make or declare sacred; to ordain to a sacred office
"The priest <u>consecrated</u> the newborn by baptizing her with holy water."
consecration (n.)
sacrare to make sacred; to dedicate

execrate v. to feel or express great loathing for; to swear
"The Nazis <u>execrated</u> gypsies and consequently tried to exterminate them."
exsecrari to curse; to detest

sacrament n. a religious ceremony or ritual regarded as imparting divine grace, such as baptism, the Eucharist, etc.
"The seven <u>sacraments</u> or holy rites instituted by Roman Catholics are described in the New Testament."
sacramentum solemn oath; a sacrament; a guaranty

sacred adj. connected with a deity and so deserving veneration; holy
"The holy grail is the legendary <u>sacred</u> cup used at the Last Supper."
sacer, sacra sacred

sacrilege n. violation or misuse of something regarded as sacred or as having great value
"The defacing of church property is considered <u>sacrilege</u>."

sacrilegious (n.)
sacrilegium sacrilege < *sacra* sacred + *legere* to take possession of

sanctify
v. to consecrate; to make legitimate or binding by religious sanction
"A marriage may be <u>sanctified</u> by a minister's blessing."
sanctity (n.)
sanctus holy

sanctimonious
adj. making a show of being morally superior or more pious than another
"A <u>sanctimonious</u> person is often derisively described as 'holier-than-thou.'"
sanctus holy

sanction
n. a threatened penalty for disobeying a law or rule; official permission or approval for an action
"Although his boss had *sanctioned* his sales plan, when it failed to produce results, she *sanctioned* him by cutting his bonus."
sanctus holy

sanctity
n. holiness; saintliness; ultimate importance and inviolability
"The <u>sanctity</u> of the church was violated when the Guatemalan Army forced the villagers inside, then set the building on fire."
sanctus holy

sanctum
n. a sacred place; a private place or retreat
"The scholar treated his library as a <u>sanctum</u> for his precious hours of solitary reading."
sancire to ordain; to dedicate < *sanctus* holy

presage
v. to be a sign or warning of (an imminent event)
n. an omen or portent
"A thunderstorm is <u>presaged</u> by the return to shelter of bees and other flying insects."
praesagire to portend: *prae-* before + *sagax, sagacis* perceptive; acute

sagacious
adj. having or showing good judgment
"Solomon is portrayed as a wise ruler and <u>sagacious</u> judge."
sagax, sagacis perceptive; acute

sapient
adj. wise
"He was full of <u>sapient</u> advice for students applying to college."
sapiens wise < *sapere* to be wise

assail
v. to make a concerted or violent attack on
"Armor-piercing English longbow arrows <u>assailed</u> the French knights at Agincourt."
ad- toward + *salire* to leap

assault
n. a violent attack; a concerted attempt to do something demanding
v. to make an attack on
"The bank robber could not be charged with <u>assault</u> since the teller did not

	feel threatened." *ad-* toward + *salire* to leap
exult	**v.** to show or feel triumphant elation "West Point cadets <u>exult</u> at graduation by tossing their caps – some with money tucked inside – into the air for children to catch." *exultation (n.)* *exsilire* to spring forth; to bound upward: *ex-* out + *salire* to leap
insult	**v.** to speak about or treat with disrespect or abuse **n.** an offensive remark or action "The victim suffered more from the racial <u>insults</u> than from the beating." *insultare* to jump or trample on: *in-* against + *salire* to leap
saline	**adj.** containing or impregnated with salt **n.** a saline solution "By dint of their salt content, seawater and blood are <u>saline</u> fluids." *sal* salt
consanguinity	**n.** relation by descent from a common ancestor; a close connection "An adopted child usually shares no <u>consanguinity</u> with its parents, unless they are aunts and uncles or grandparents." *consanguineus* blood relation: *con-* together + *sanguis, sanguinis* blood; family
sanguine	**adj.** cheerfully optimistic or confident; of a reddish complexion; bloody **n.** a blood red color "Thanks to unprecedented financial growth, the college graduate was <u>sanguine</u> about his job prospects." *sanguis, sanguinis* blood; family

Exercise A

Fill in the blanks in the sentences below with the correct form of a word in the scroll above.

1. The _____ of the Olympic games has been repeatedly threatened in recent decades by doping scandals.

2. Ben Franklin, a _____ gentleman, once said, "A bird in the hand is worth two in the bush."

3. At Agincourt, Frenchmen showed their middle fingers to the British longbowmen as a threat to cut off their fingers so they could no longer shoot, and the gesture has since become a common _____.

4. Jerusalem is a hotbed of conflict, in part due to the three monotheistic religions practiced there, all of whose adherents consider the city _____.

5. The rowdy man _____ his listeners' ears with loud insults and obscenities.

6. The girl, praised by her teacher as an example to all, gave her classmates a _____ smile.

7. During emergencies in which the patient has lost a lot of blood, paramedics maintain blood pressure by pumping a _____ solution into a vein.

8. The bishop was coming next week to _____ the new baptismal font, donated by the parishioners.

9. The word _____ is related to the term for the human species – *homo sapiens*.

10. A Christian baby receives the _____ of baptism.

11. At the Battle of the Somme in World War I, Sir Douglas Haig ordered a direct _____ on German positions, resulting in 40,000 British casualties during the first day of conflict.

12. The United Nations has a policy to _____ any country that does not comply with international agreements.

13. When his owners come home after vacation, Wishbone _____ by barking and chasing his tail.

14. Some Muslims feel that the occupation by Americans of parts of Saudi Arabia is a _____, because the troops are so close to the holy city of Mecca.

15. He was quite _____ about his marriage, and his new wife seemed equally optimistic.

16. Some conservative commentators _____ pro wrestling's glorification of sex and violence, but their protests have only served to increase its popularity.

17. Red Cloud interpreted his dream of white rain falling from the sky as _____ a Native American victory.

18. While some artists cloister themselves in a personal _____ to reduce interruptions and distill their thoughts, others look for inspiration by exploring the world.

19. Legend holds that to ward off evil spirits, a priest must _____ holy water.

20. He shares _____ with his half-brother, but not with his step-sister.

Exercise B

Match the word with the letter of its definition.

1. ___ assail
2. ___ assault
3. ___ consanguinity
4. ___ consecrate
5. ___ execrate
6. ___ exult
7. ___ insult
8. ___ presage
9. ___ sacrament
10. ___ sacred
11. ___ sacrilege
12. ___ sagacious
13. ___ saline
14. ___ sanctify
15. ___ sanctimonious
16. ___ sanction
17. ___ sanctity
18. ___ sanctum
19. ___ sanguine
20. ___ sapient

a) a religious ceremony or ritual
b) to make or declare sacred
c) violation or misuse of something sacred
d) to speak about or treat with disrespect or abuse
e) containing or impregnated with salt
f) to consecrate
g) holiness, saintliness
h) to make a concerted or violent attack on
i) having or showing good judgment
j) confident and optimistic in outlook; bloody
k) to penalize for disobeying a law or rule; to approve
l) a violent attack
m) wise
n) a sacred or private place
o) to be a sign or warning of; a portent
p) to feel or express great loathing for
q) descent from a common ancestor
r) to show or feel triumphant elation
s) holy; connected with a deity
t) making a show of being morally superior

Exercise C

Solve the crossword puzzle.

Across
3. Containing or impregnated with salt. 4. A penalty for disobeying a law or rule; official permission or approval for an action. 7. Having or showing good judgment. 10. To make or declare sacred; to ordain to a sacred office. 11. Cheerfully optimistic. 12. To speak about or treat with disrespect or abuse. 16. A violent attack; a concerted attempt to do something demanding. 18. To consecrate; to make legitimate or binding by religious sanction. 19. To show or feel triumphant elation. 20. A religious ceremony or ritual regarded as imparting divine grace, such as baptism, the Eucharist, etc.

Down
1. Descent from a common ancestor. 2. Violation or misuse of something regarded as sacred or having great value. 5. To be a sign or warning of (an imminent event). 6. A sacred place; a private place. 8. Connected with a deity and so deserving veneration; holy. 9. Wise. 13. Making a show of being morally superior or more pious than others. 14. Holiness; saintliness; ultimate importance and inviolability. 15. To feel or express great loathing for. 17. To make a concerted or violent attack on.

Lesson XIV
satis, scintilla, scrib/script, sect, secut

SATIS
enough

SCINTILLA
spark

SCRIB, SCRIPT
to write

SECT
to cut

SECUT
to follow

satiate, scintilla, ascribe, conscript, inscribe, manuscript, prescribe, proscribe, scripture, subscribe, transcribe, bisect, dissect, segment, consecutive, consequence, non sequitur, sequel, sequence, subsequent

Word Definitions

satiate
    v. to satisfy fully
    adj. fully satisfying
    "Tea and hors d'oeuvres at midafternoon failed to satiate his hunger."
    satiare to satisfy; to nourish < *satis* enough

scintilla
    n. a tiny trace or amount
    "There was not a scintilla of evidence against her, and they had to let her go."
    scintilla spark

ascribe
    v. to attribute something to
    "Some scholars argue that the plays ascribed to Shakespeare were actually written by someone else."
    ascribere to state in writing; to insert: *ad-* to + *scribere* to write

conscript
    v. to draft into the armed forces; to compel someone to do (something)
    n. someone forced into service
    "American forces in Vietnam were a mix of volunteers and conscripts who had been drafted."
    conscribere to enroll; to enlist: *con-* together + *scribere* to write

inscribe
    v. to write on or carve into a surface, especially as a formal or permanent record
    "The stone pillars at Karnak are inscribed with hieroglyphs."
    inscription (n.)
    inscribere to write on; to brand: *in-* in-, into + *scribere* to write

manuscript	**n.** a handwritten book, document, or piece of music; a text submitted for publication "'The slush pile' is how publishers refer to unsolicited <u>manuscripts</u>." *manuscriptus* handwritten: *manu* hand + *scriptus* written
prescribe	**v.** to advise and authorize the use of, especially in writing; to state authoritatively that something should be done in a particular way "The doctor <u>prescribed</u> an antibiotic for her bronchitis." *prescription (n.)* *praescribere* to direct in writing: *prae-* before + *scribere* to write
proscribe	**v.** to forbid, especially by law "Bicycles, horses, and hitchhikers are <u>proscribed</u> on interstate highways." *proscribere* to proscribe; to post (publicly): *pro-* before + *scribere* to write
scripture	**n.** the sacred writings of Christianity contained in the Bible; any writing or dictum treated as authoritative and to be followed without question "Mothers in the 1950s treated Dr. Spock's "Baby and Child Care" as <u>scripture</u>." *scriptura* writing; scripture < *scribere* to write
subscribe	**v.** to arrange to receive something regularly, especially a periodical, by paying in advance; to agree with an idea or proposal "Christians <u>subscribe</u> to a belief in resurrection after death." *subscription (n.)* subscribere to subscribe: *sub-* under + *scribere* to write
transcribe	**v.** to put into written or printed form; to copy; to arrange a piece of music for a different instrument or instruments; to write out in another language "A stenographer <u>transcribes</u> dictation into shorthand, then typewritten copy." *transcription (n.)* *transcribere* to copy; to transfer: *trans-* across + *scribere* to write
bisect	**v.** to divide into two parts, usually equal "The equator is an imaginary line that <u>bisects</u> the earth between its poles." *bisection (n.)* *bi-* two + *secare* to cut
dissect	**v.** to methodically cut up (an animal) in order to study its internal parts; to analyze in minute detail "'The Decline and Fall of the Roman Empire' <u>dissects</u> the causes of Rome's demise." *dissection (n.)* *dissecare* to cut apart; to dissect: *dis-* down from + *secare* to cut
segment	**n.** each of the parts into which something is or may be divided **v.** to divide into parts "Sunday newspapers often carry inserts <u>segmented</u> by geographical area." *segmentum* a cutting; a shred < *secare* to cut

consecutive	**adj.** following continuously one after another "Only Grover Cleveland served non-<u>consecutive</u> presidential terms." *consequi* to follow closely: *con-* with + *sequi* to follow; to accompany
consequence	**n.** a result or effect "One <u>consequence</u> of his sudden heart attack was that his family was left with no means of support." *consequential (adj)* *consequi* to follow closely: *con-* with + *sequi* to follow; to accompany
non sequitur	**n.** a conclusion or statement that does not logically follow from the previous argument, statement, or line of conversation "Arguing that because his arthritis flared up before one thunderstorm, a flare-up therefore predicts thunderstorms, proved a <u>non sequitur</u>." *non* not + *sequitur* follow
sequel	**n.** a published, broadcast, or recorded work that continues the story or develops the theme of an earlier one; something that follows "<u>Sequels</u> to great movies rarely rise to the level of the original." *sequi* to follow
sequence	**n.** a particular order in which related events, movements, etc. follow each other; a set of related events or movements in a particular order "The <u>sequence</u> of episodes in Joyce's *Ulysses* mirrors Homer's *Odyssey*." *sequential (adj.)* *sequi* to follow
subsequent	**adj.** coming after something in time "John Adams was president immediately <u>subsequent</u> to Washington." *subsequi* to follow after: *sub-* under, below + *sequi* to follow

Exercise A

Fill in the blanks in the sentences below with the correct form of a word in the scroll above.

1. The Rosetta Stone, _____ in three languages, has aided in the deciphering of Egyptian hieroglyphics.

2. The movie *Rocky* was such a blockbuster that _____ became inevitable.

3. Part of high school biology is _____ a frog to study its anatomy.

4. The disastrous box office failure of *Gigli* foreshadowed the _____ breakup of Jen and Ben.

5. The Dead Sea scrolls include _____ from the Hebrew Bible.

6. The firefly gave off only a _____ of light after capture.

7. During monsoon season in Bangladesh, it can rain for more than 30 _____ days, but nearly every building is built on stilts.

8. He loves those chocolate oranges that you can break into _____.

9. In Puritan societies, the church _____ singing, dancing, and merry-making because those activities distracted the soul from contemplation of God.

10. She sent her _____ off to the publisher with a sigh of relief that the ordeal – of the first draft, anyway – was over.

11. The library decided to _____ a wide range of literary magazines.

12. Before antibiotics were widely available, doctors _____ sulfa drugs for dangerous bacterial infections.

13. Vampires are often portrayed as vicious creatures that must kill and drink human blood in order to _____ their hunger.

14. The equator _____ the earth into two equal halves.

15. Some _____ the fall of the Roman Empire to its incapable leadership and its immense geographical size, which together made ruling a unified nation nearly impossible.

16. The doctor dictated the notes from the examination so that the assistant could _____ them into the patient's record.

17. Johnny Knoxville subjects himself to unimaginable physical anguish and takes outrageous risks with little regard for the _____.

18. Thirty-five years ago, Jim Pratt was a young _____ willing to fight for his country.

19. The _____ of events that comprise Freddie Prinze Jr.'s rise to fame are utterly incomprehensible.

20. The use of a _____ can confuse the conversation.

Exercise B

Match the word with the letter of its definition.

1. ___ ascribe
2. ___ bisect
3. ___ conscript
4. ___ consecutive
5. ___ consequence
6. ___ dissect
7. ___ inscribe
8. ___ manuscript
9. ___ non sequitur
10. ___ prescribe
11. ___ proscribe
12. ___ satiate
13. ___ scintilla
14. ___ scripture
15. ___ segment
16. ___ sequel
17. ___ sequence
18. ___ subscribe
19. ___ subsequent
20. ___ transcribe

a) following in time
b) to write on or carve into a surface
c) fully satisfied
d) to arrange to receive something periodically; to agree with a theory or view
e) text of a book or a written piece of music
f) to attribute something to
g) the sacred writings of Christianity in the Bible
h) to draft into the armed forces
i) a book, movie, or broadcast that continues a prior story
j) a particular order in which related events, movements, etc. follow each other
k) to put into written or printed form
l) a result or effect
m) to divide into two parts
n) each of the parts into which something can be divided
o) to advise and authorize the use of (esp. medication)
p) following continuously in sequence
q) to methodically cut up for scientific study
r) a tiny trace or amount; a spark
s) to forbid, especially by law
t) a conclusion or statement that does not logically follow

Exercise C

Across

4. To attribute something to. 7. Coming after something in time. 9. To divide into two parts. 11. To draft into the armed forces. 12. To put into written or printed form; to arrange a piece of music for a different instrument or ensemble. 14. To write on or carve into a surface, especially as a formal or permanent record. 15. To methodically cut up in order to study its internal parts; to analyze in minute detail. 16. Fully satisfied. 17. The sacred writings of Christianity contained in the Bible. 18. To advise and authorize the use of, especially in writing; to state authoritatively that something should be done in a particular way. 19. Each of the parts into which something is or may be divided.

Down

1. To forbid, especially by law. 2. A particular order in which related events, movements, etc. follow each other; a set of related events movements, etc. in a particular order. 3. A handwritten book, document, or piece of music; a text submitted for publication. 5. A tiny trace or amount. 6. To arrange to receive something regularly, especially a periodical, by paying advance; to agree with an idea or proposal. 7. A published broadcast or recorded work that continues the story or develops the theme of an earlier one. 8. A conclusion or statement that does not logically follow from the previous argument, statement, or conversation. 10. A result or effect. 13. Following continuously, in sequence.

Test 2

Choose the correct meaning for the underlined vocabulary word in each sentence.

1. "Nothing walks, or creeps, or grows, or exists, which must not in turn arise and walk before him as <u>exponent</u> of his meaning."

   Essays, Second Series by Ralph Waldo Emerson

   (a) one who deceives   (b) one who promotes an idea
   (c) one who interchanges   (d) one who labors   (e) one who expels

2. "Between the two lies the broad belt, of comparative desert, which is the scene of this tale, appearing to <u>interpose</u> a barrier to the progress of the American people westward."

   The Prairie by James Fenimore Cooper

   (a) force to be accepted   (b) remove from power
   (c) introduce between things   (d) interchange   (e) expel from a country

3. "Captain Hull then took a key from his girdle, unlocked the chest, and lifted its <u>ponderous</u> lid."

   Grandfather's Chair by Nathaniel Hawthorne

   (a) measured   (b) unimportant   (c) dominant   (d) heavy
   (e) thoughtful

4. "The Rivers joined together to complain to the Sea, saying, "Why is it that when we flow into your tides so <u>potable</u> and sweet, you work in us such a change, and make us salty and unfit to drink?"

   Fables by Aesop

   (a) easily carried   (b) drinkable   (c) trustworthy   (d) imported
   (e) term of office

5. "'Well, of all the--' ejaculated the man, with an oddly <u>impotent</u> gesture."

   Pollyanna by Eleanor H. Porter

   (a) convenient   (b) preying   (c) influential   (d) powerful
   (e) helpless

6. "I come down here, for instance, and I find a mighty <u>potentate</u> exacting homage."
Bleak House by Charles Dickens

(a) opportunist   (b) ruler   (c) priest   (d) predator
(e) body guard

7. "Letters of <u>reprisal</u> were granted, and a war ensued, which in its consequences overthrew all the alliances that but 20 years before had been formed with sanguine expectations of the most beneficial fruits."
Federalist Papers by Alexander Hamilton

(a) retaliation   (b) dejection   (c) compression   (d) censure
(e) reprimand

8. "How comes all this, if there be not something <u>puissant</u> in whaling?"
Moby Dick by Herman Mellvile

(a) unimportant   (b) powerful   (c) objectionable   (d) powerless
(e) impotent

9. "With an irritable toss of his head he wheeled suddenly toward the west, as though by turning his back upon the fast disappearing plane he might <u>expunge</u> thoughts of its passengers from his memory."
Tarzan the Untamed by Edgar Rice Burroughs

(a) attack   (b) disapprove   (c) erase   (d) dispute   (e) reprove

10. "It is a hardy question, fair sir and Boss, since it doth go far to <u>impugn</u> the wisdom of even our holy Mother Church herself.
A Connecticut Yankee by Mark Twain

(a) challenge   (b) rebuke   (c) convey   (d) reprimand   (e) disapprove

11. "This obligation cost her so much that she consulted her director, the Abbe Couturier, upon the subject of this honest but <u>puerile</u> civility."
An Old Maid by Honore de Balzac

(a) old   (b) punitive   (c) unprincipled   (d) childish   (e) belligerent

12. "The old prince, like all fathers indeed, was exceedingly <u>punctilious</u> on the score of the honor and reputation of his daughters."
Anna Karenina by Leo Tolstoy

(a) argumentative   (b) meticulous   (c) caustic   (d) painful   (e) informal

13. "From the first, my fellow pupils used to tease and deride and mock me whenever I was saying my lessons."
Poor Folk by Fyodor Dostoyevsky

    (a) ridicule   (b) justify   (c) pray   (d) arrange in a pattern   (e) rebel

14. "The wolf of the forest is not more rapacious for his prey than that man is greedy of gold; and yet his glidings into wealth are subtle as the movements of a serpent."
The Pioneers by James Fenimore Cooper

    (a) absurd   (b) voracious   (c) reasonable   (d) reformed
    (e) conforming to standards

15. "And at the joyous rapture of the voice, more than one pair of eyes in the room brimmed hot with sudden tears."
Pollyanna by Eleanor H. Porter

    (a) logic   (b) instruction   (c) violence   (d) laughter   (e) ecstasy

16. "It is the law of nature – no man-made law can abrogate the laws of God."
The Son Of Tarzan by Edgar Rice Burroughs

    (a) claim   (b) invalidate   (c) question aggressively   (d) understand entirely
    (e) break out of

17. "The whole substance of human authority was centered in the simple doctrine of royal prerogative, the origin of which was always traced in theory to divine institution."
Orations by John Quincy Adams

    (a) control   (b) importance   (c) privilege   (d) question
    (e) principle

18. "So alarming did the state of my finances become, that I soon realized that I must either leave the metropolis and rusticate somewhere in the country, or that I must make a complete alteration in my style of living."
A Study In Scarlet by Sir Arthur Conan Doyle

    (a) live in the country   (b) disturb or interrupt   (c) perform manual labor
    (d) break continuity of   (e) burst suddenly

19. "Fanny coloured, and doubted at first what to say; when, hoping to assail her on her vulnerable side, she presently answered…"
Mansfield Park by Jane Austen

    (a) warn   (b) demand   (c) consecrate   (d) attack   (e) seduce

20. "Jane's frame of mind was naturally depressed and timorous, having been affected by Miranda's gloomy <u>presages</u> of evil to come."
Rebecca Of Sunnybrook Farm by Kate Douglas Wiggin

   (a) sacred places (b) saintliness (c) rituals (d) violations
   (e) warnings

21. "Coiler made admiring comments on their eyes, noses, and legs – a <u>sagacious</u> way of improving their minds."
Great Expectations by Charles Dickens

   (a) prudent, shrewd (b) holy, sacrosanct (c) supercilious, flighty
   (d) unorthodox, risky (e) bloodthirsty, grim

22. "He was donned in his Sunday garments, with his most <u>sanctimonious</u> and sourest face, and, holding his hat in one hand, and his stick in the other, he proceeded to clean his shoes on the mat."
Wuthering Heights by Emily Bronte

   (a) wise, kind (b) morally superior (c) holy (d) troublesome
   (e) bitter

23. "I think that in those days I never forgot the fact of my elevation for five <u>consecutive</u> minutes."
The Mirror of the Sea by Joseph Conrad

   (a) calm (b) motivating (c) sequential (d) coming after
   (e) later

24. "I shall <u>satiate</u> my ardent curiosity with the sight of a part of the world never before visited, and may tread a land never before imprinted by the foot of man."
Frankenstein by Mary Shelley

   (a) investigate (b) portray regularly (c) forbid legally
   (d) fully satisfy (e) analyze in detail

25. "As the first part of *An Old-Fashioned Girl* was written in 1869, the demand for a <u>sequel</u>, in beseeching little letters that made refusal impossible, rendered it necessary to carry my heroine boldly forward some six or seven years into the future."
An Old-Fashioned Girl by Louisa May Alcott

   (a) dichotomy (b) continuation (c) conclusion
   (d) illogical sequence (e) unequal distribution

Lesson XV

sed-/sid-, senis, sens-/sent-, simil-/simul

SED-, SID-	**SENIS**	**SENS-, SENT-**	**SIMIL-, SIMUL**
to sit	old	to think, to feel	like, similar

assiduous, dissident, residual, sedative, sedentary, session, senile, assent, consensus, dissent, presentiment, resent, sensory, sensual, sentiment, assimilate, dissimilar, simile, simulate, simultaneous

Word Definitions

assiduous adj. showing great care and perseverance
"Darwin did assiduous research on pigeon breeding in developing his theory of evolution."
assidere to sit in council; to settle: *a-* to + *sidere* to sit (a variant of *sedere*)

dissident n. a person who opposes official policy
"In Stalinist Russia, communist dissidents were summarily rounded up and shot."
dissidere to sit apart; to disagree: *dis-* down from + *sidere* to sit

residual adj. left over; remaining after the greater part or quantity has been removed or subtracted
n. a residual quantity; a royalty paid to a performer or writer for a repeat of a play, show, or advertisement
"There were residual traces of gunpowder on the shooter's fingertips."
residere to be left over; to remain; to reside: *re-* again + *sidere* to sit

sedative adj. promoting calm or inducing sleep
n. a sleep-inducing drug
"A glass of warm milk before bedtime is a sufficient sedative for many."
sedate (v.)
sedare to settle; to calm down (a variant of *sedere* to sit)

sedentary adj. tending to spend much time seated or in one place; not nomadic
"Doctors caution against the sedentary lifestyle of computer geeks."
sedentis sitting (present participle of *sedere* to sit)

session	**n.** a period devoted to a particular activity; a meeting of a deliberative or judicial body to conduct its business; the part of a year or a day during which teaching takes place in a school "Cabinet meetings are conducted in <u>sessions</u> closed to the media." *sessus* seated (past participle of the verb *sedere* to sit)
senile	**adj.** having the weakness or diseases of old age; forgetful or mentally incapacitated because of age "Guardians are often appointed for <u>senile</u> nursing home residents." *senex, senis* old man; aged
assent	**n.** an expression of approval or agreement **v.** to express approval; to agree to "In most cultures, a nod is a gesture of <u>assent</u>." *assentire* to agree; to comply with: *ad-* toward + *sentire* to feel; to perceive
consensus	**n.** general or unanimous agreement "The subcommittee reached a positive <u>consensus</u> and forwarded the nomination." *consensus* agreement; consent; harmony < *consentire* to agree: *con-* with + *sentire* to feel; to perceive
dissent	**v.** to express disagreement with a prevailing view or official decision **n.** the holding or expression of a dissenting view "The measure was adopted by a 99-1 vote; Rep. Ronald Dellums was the lone voice of <u>dissent</u>." *dissentire* to differ in sentiment: *dis-* down from + *sentire* to feel; to perceive
presentiment	**n.** an intuitive feeling or foreboding about the future "She had a <u>presentiment</u> that when she returned from Iraq, her fiance would tell her he had fallen in love with someone else." *praesentire* to perceive beforehand: *prae-* before + *sentire* to feel; to perceive
resent	**v.** to feel bitterness, indignation, or jealousy toward "Those who <u>resented</u> Alexander's power may have tried to poison him." *resentment (n.)* *re-* back + *sentire* to feel; to perceive
sensory	**adj.** relating to sensation or the senses; simulating the senses "Bank vaults have <u>sensory</u> devices to detect heat, motion, pressure, and sound." *sentire* to feel; to perceive
sensual	**adj.** relating to the physical senses, especially as a source of pleasure; arousing physical gratification "A chiropractor's massage is therapeutic; a lover's massage is more <u>sensual</u>." *sentire* to feel; to perceive

sentiment	**n.** a view, opinion, or feeling; exaggerated and self-indulgent feelings of tenderness, sadness, or nostalgia "The least reminder of her late husband triggered an outpouring of <u>sentiment</u>." *sentire* to feel
assimilate	**v.** to take in and fully understand; to absorb and digest food; to regard as or become similar "The exhaustive list of geometric formulas was difficult to <u>assimilate</u> and remember." *assimilis* similar; closely resembling: *ad-* to + *similis* like
dissimilar	**adj.** not alike; different "Men and women tend to have <u>dissimilar</u> movie preferences." *dissimilis* unlike; different: *dis-* (expressing negation) + *similis* like
simile	**n.** a figure of speech involving the comparison of one thing with another thing of a different kind. "Here's an example of a <u>simile</u>: 'She was like a butterfly, flitting from man to man, feeding on the nectar of their admiration.'" *similis* like
simulate	**v.** to imitate or to reproduce the appearance, character, or conditions of "The initial symptoms of a heart attack can <u>simulate</u> heartburn or the flu." *simulation (n.)* *simulare* to copy, to represent (a variant of *similare*)
simultaneous	**adj.** occurring, operating, or done at the same time "Thomas Jefferson and John Adams died almost <u>simultaneously</u> on July 4, 1826." *simul* at the same time; likewise; at once

Exercise A

Fill in the blanks in the sentences below with the correct form of a word in the scroll above.

1. School was not in _____ when the story of the murders broke, so it was difficult for reporters to reach students and teachers for comment.

2. Internet-based phone service has become so good that there is no longer an audible speech delay or echo; transmission seems _____ with reception.

3. Without our body's _____ organs, we would be unable to perceive the world in which we live.

4. People tend to _____ giving up their hard-earned money to pay income taxes.

5. The world's most respected environmental scientists have reached a _____ on a major cause of global warming: human activity.

6. Parallel increases in high-calorie foods and _____ jobs have led to a rise in obesity.

7. NASA space camp has computers that _____ space flight, giving students the opportunity to "experience" space travel.

8. Demonstrators _____ from the governor's views on gay marriage by picketing the Statehouse.

9. In a Milky Way commercial, a man gets more _____ pleasure from a candy bar than a massage.

10. Years of toil finally paid off for the _____ scientist when she developed the first drug used to combat the progress of Alzheimer's disease.

11. The Democratic and Republican proposals for shoring up the Social Security issue are not too _____ , so there's hope they will agree on a bill.

12. Even though Massachusetts is a heavily Democratic state, the Republican presidential candidate, George Bush, _____ to a debate in Boston.

13. Uneasy because of a _____ of disaster, the custodian moved the ladder just before the heavy chandelier fell.

14. Peyton is anxious to play football again, but first the doctor wants to ensure that he isn't suffering any _____ effects from last week's concussion.

15. Research has shown that behavioral therapy is as effective as prescription _____ for those suffering from anxiety disorders.

16. Although the elderly man had warned that aliens were about to invade the small Utah town, his words of caution were dismissed as _____ ramblings.

17. As a teenager, Barack Obama was sometimes troubled by questions about his identity, for he was never completely _____ into either the African-American or white communities.

18. An upbeat piece of action music would convey the wrong _____ at most funerals, but seemed appropriate for the Hollywood stuntman's memorial service.

19. Being a _____ is lonely and often exhausting, which explains why many aging radicals "sell out" and join the political mainstream.

20. A _____ is as useful in literature as a shovel is in a garden.

Exercise B

Match the word with the letter of its definition.

1. ___ assent
2. ___ assiduous
3. ___ assimilate
4. ___ consensus
5. ___ dissent
6. ___ dissident
7. ___ dissimilar
8. ___ presentiment
9. ___ resent
10. ___ residual
11. ___ sedative
12. ___ sedentary
13. ___ senile
14. ___ sentiment
15. ___ session
16. ___ sensory
17. ___ sensual
18. ___ simile
19. ___ simulate
20. ___ simultaneous

a) general or unanimous agreement
b) tending to spend much time seated or inactive
c) occurring or done at the same time
d) a drug promoting calm or inducing sleep
e) to imitate the appearance or conditions of
f) a period devoted to a particular activity
g) showing great care and perseverance
h) arousing physical gratification
i) having the weakness or diseases of old age
j) not similar; unlike
k) to absorb and digest (food, an idea, etc.)
l) remaining after the greater part has gone
m) to express approval or agreement
n) relating to sensation or the senses
o) a comparative figure of speech
p) an intuitive foreboding about the future
q) to feel bitterness, indignation, or jealousy toward
r) feelings of tenderness, sadness, or nostalgia
s) a person who opposes official policy
t) to express disagreement with a prevailing view or official decision

Exercise C

Solve the crossword puzzle.

Across
1. Unlike. 3. A period devoted to a particular activity; a meeting of a deliberative or judicial body; the part of a school year or day when teaching takes place. 7. Occurring, operating, or done at the same time. 11. Relating to sensation or the senses. 13. To feel bitterness toward. 14. Showing great care and perseverance. 15. A figure of speech involving the comparison of one thing with another thing of a different kind. 16. To express disagreement with a prevailing view or official decision. 17. Expression of approval or agreement. 18. Promoting calm or inducing sleep. 19. To imitate or reproduce the appearance, character, or conditions of.

Down
2. Left over; remaining after the greater part or quantity has been removed. 3. Forgetful or mentally incapacitated due to old age. 4. To take in and fully understand; to absorb and digest food; to become similar to. 5. A person who opposes official policy. 6. General or unanimous agreement. 8. A view, opinion, or feeling; exaggerated and self-indulgent feelings of tenderness, sadness, or nostalgia. 9. An intuitive feeling or foreboding about the future. 10. Relating to the physical senses, especially as a source of pleasure; arousing physical gratification. 12. Tending to spend much time seated or inactive.

Lesson XVI
sol, solv/solut, somn, son

SOL-   **SOLV, SOLUT**   **SOMN**   **SON**
alone   to loosen   to sleep   sound

desolate, soliloquy, solipsism, solitude, solo, absolute, absolve, dissolute, dissolve, resolution, resolve, solute, solvent, insomnia, somnolent, resonate, sonar, sonic, supersonic, unison

Word Definitions

desolate   **adj.** giving an impression of bleak and dismal emptiness; utterly wretched and unhappy
"Napoleon spent his last years in desolate exile on the island of Elba."
desolation (n.)
desolare to abandon; to empty of people < *de-* down, from + *solus, sola* alone

soliloquy   **n.** a solo speech (especially in a play) during which someone speaks his thoughts aloud, unheard by others
"Alone on stage, Macbeth airs his sorrowful thoughts in a soliloquy."
solus, sola alone + *loqui* to speak

solipsism   **n.** the view or theory that the self is all that can be known to exist
"She believed in solipsism, while he believed in the separate existence of the physical universe."
solus, sola alone + *ipse* self

solitude   **n.** the state of being alone
"A hermit prefers a life of solitude."
solus, sola alone

solo   **n.** a piece of music, song, or dance for one performer; an unaccompanied flight by a pilot
adj./adv. for or done by one person
v. to perform solo
"'O solo mio!' is a well known operatic solo popularized by Enrico

Caruso."
solus, sola alone

absolute
adj. total; not relative or comparative
n. a value or principle regarded as universally valid or able to be viewed without relation to other things
"One philosophy insists on <u>absolutes</u>; its counterpart holds that all things are relative."
absolutus absolute < *absolvere* to set free; to acquit: *ab-* from + *solvere* to loosen; to unbind

absolve
v. to declare someone free of guilt or responsibility
"A rock solid alibi <u>absolved</u> the suspect, who was subsequently released."
absolvere to set free; to acquit: *ab-* from + *solvere* to loosen; to unbind

dissolute
adj. overindulgent in sensual pleasures
"Attila died after a <u>dissolute</u> wedding night of drinking and sensual celebration."
dissolutus disconnected; dissolved; destroyed

dissolve
v. to become or to cause to become incorporated into a liquid so as to form a solution; to formally end an assembly or a marriage
n. an instance of dissolving from one image or scene in a film to another
"Annulment is the Catholic alternative to divorce, as a means to <u>dissolve</u> a marriage."
dissolvere to disconnect; to dissolve; to destroy: *dis-* apart + *solvere* to loosen; to unbind

resolution
n. the quality of being decided or determined; a firm or forward-looking decision; the settlement of a problem or dispute
"Many New Year's <u>resolutions</u> to change bad habits are quickly broken."
resolute (adj.)
resolutio unraveling or resolution (of a puzzle): *re-* (expressing intensive force) + *solutio* weakening; loosening

resolve
v. to settle or find a solution to; to decide firmly on a course of action; to take on a clear form when seen more closely
n. determination
"A detective's task is to follow clues and evidence to <u>resolve</u> a crime."
resolvere to loosen; to release: *re-* (expressing intensive force) + *solvere* to loosen; to unbind

solute
n. the minor component in a solution, dissolved in the solvent
"Fake maple syrup typically uses a sugar <u>solute</u> dissolved in flavored water."
solvere to loosen; to unbind

solvent
adj. having assets in excess of liabilities; not bankrupt
n. the liquid in which a solute is dissolved to form a solution
"His company was barely <u>solvent</u>, so he filed for bankruptcy protection."
solvere to loosen; to unbind

insomnia	**n.** habitual sleeplessness; difficulty falling asleep or getting back to sleep "Insomnia is rarely a problem for cats, who typically nap 18 hours a day." *insomnis* sleepless
somnolent	**adj.** sleepy; drowsy "A lullaby lulled the already somnolent baby to sleep." *somnus, somni* sleep
resonate	**v.** to continue ringing or reverberating; to evoke enduring images, memories, or emotions "A yodel resonates in the echoing Alps." *resonare* to resound: *re-* back, again + *sonare* to sound
sonar	**n.** a system for the detection of objects under water, based on the emission and measured reflection of sound pulses; the method of echolocation used in air or water by animals such as bats and whales "A car equipped with sonar automatically stays a safe distance behind another vehicle." abbreviation for *sound navigation and ranging* < *sonare* to sound
sonic	**adj.** relating to or using sound waves "Sonic waves travel faster in water than air." *sonus, soni* sound, noise
supersonic	**adj.** involving or denoting a speed greater than the speed of sound "Traveling faster than sound, the Concorde provides supersonic transport." *super* above, over + *sonus, soni* sound, noise
unison	**n.** simultaneous group action or utterance "The choir usually sang in parts, but performed the Gregorian chant in unison." *uni-* one + *sonus, soni* sound

Exercise A

Fill in the blanks in the sentences below with the correct form of a word in the scroll above.

1. Charles Lindbergh was greeted with great acclaim in Paris after he became the first person to fly _____ across the Atlantic.

2. Although he played with a fury not seen since Jimi Hendrix, the teenager electric guitar player's riffs were nearly inaudible without _____ amplifiers.

3. To make caramel sauce, you must first _____ brown sugar in butter.

4. The submarine's _____ system malfunctioned, leaving it without an underwater navigational system, so it was forced to surface.

5. In Shakespeare's *Hamlet*, the prince delivers the famous _____ in which he asks himself "To be or not to be – that is the question."

6. A _____ like Goo-Gone is often used to remove sticky residues from various surfaces.

7. His _____ and sometimes illegal behavior caused him to lose his job, his marriage, and his home.

8. _____ is a common sleep disorder that can be caused by a combination of stress, poor diet, genetics, and lack of exercise.

9. The judge admonished the jurors to be _____ sure of the suspect's guilt before bringing in a conviction.

10. Their marriage is difficult because she loves going out and entertaining, while her husband prefers _____ .

11. Jason decided to _____ his recurring problems with spyware by installing anti-virus software.

12. When added to water, the _____ dissolves.

13. The priest hearing confessions _____ the boy of his sins.

14. Although Mrs. Waterhouse insisted that she was enthralled by her son's soccer game, her _____ yawn belied her true feelings.

15. Marcy's New Year's _____ is to be more generous to her brother.

16. Antarctica is so _____ that one can travel hundreds of miles without encountering any type of life form.

17. The women gave Anita Hill a standing ovation and chanted her first name in _____ for her courageous testimony during Clarence Thomas's Supreme Court confirmation hearing.

18. _____ – the belief that the self is all that can be known to exist – can be confused with egotism, which is the quality of being excessively conceited.

19. Be careful what you say in a church or other large, open room; even the smallest whispers tend to _____ throughout the building.

20. _____ speeds are not only possible, but are accomplished every day by jets across the world.

Exercise B

Match the word with the letter of its definition.

1. ___ absolute
2. ___ absolve
3. ___ desolate
4. ___ dissolute
5. ___ dissolve
6. ___ insomnia
7. ___ resolution
8. ___ resolve
9. ___ resonate
10. ___ soliloquy
11. ___ solipsism
12. ___ solitude
13. ___ solo
14. ___ solute
15. ___ solvent
16. ___ somnolent
17. ___ sonar
18. ___ sonic
19. ___ supersonic
20. ___ unison

a) sleepy; drowsy
b) an individual musical performance
c) habitual sleeplessness
d) the minor component in a solution
e) relating to or using sound waves
f) a speech in which someone expresses his thoughts aloud, unheard by others (especially in a play)
g) a system for the detection of objects under water
h) a value regarded as universally valid
i) to evoke enduring memories, images, or emotions
j) to become incorporated into a liquid
k) the state of being alone
l) overindulgent in sensual pleasures
m) to declare someone free from guilt
n) a firm or forward-looking decision
o) faster than the speed of sound
p) giving an impression of dismal emptiness; barren or bleak
q) to settle or find a solution to
r) the liquid in which a solute is dissolved
s) simultaneous (in action, speech, or performance)
t) the view or theory that the self is all that can be known to exist

Exercise C

Solve the crossword puzzle.

Across
2. To declare someone free from guilt or responsibility. 6. Habitual sleeplessness. 11. Relating to or using sound waves. 13. The quality of being resolute; a firm or foreward-looking decision; the resolving of a problem or dispute. 14. Sleepy, drowsy. 16. Simultaneous action or utterance. 17. To become or cause to become incorporated into a liquid so as to form a solution; to formally end an assembly or marriage. 19. Having assets in excess of liabilities.

Down
1. To resound or keep ringing; to evoke enduring images, memories or emotions. 3. A system for the detection of objects under water based on the emission and measured reflection of sound pulses; the method of echolocation used in air or water by animals such as bats and whales. 4. Total; not relative or comparative. 5. A speech expressing one's thoughts aloud, with no hearers present (especially in a play). 7. The view or theory that the self is all that can be known to exist. 8. Overindulgent in sensual pleasures. 9. The state of being alone. 10. Involving or denoting a speed greater than sound. 12. The minor component in a solution, dissolved in the solvent. 15. To settle or find a solution to; to decide firmly on a course of action; to come into focus when seen more closely. 17. Giving an impression of bleak and dismal emptiness; utterly wretched and unhappy. 18. A piece of music, song, or dance for one performer; an unaccompanied flight by a pilot.

Lesson XVII
sparg-, spec-/spect-/spic-, spir-

SPARG-	SPEC-, SPECT-, SPIC-	SPIR-
to scatter	to look at	to breathe

aspersion, disperse, circumspect, despicable, introspective, perspective, specimen, spectacle, spectator, specter, spectrum, aspire, conspiracy, dispirit, expire, inspire, respiratory, spirited, spiritual, transpire

Word Definitions

aspersion   **n.** an attack on someone's (or something's) character or reputation
"The prosecutor cast <u>aspersions</u> on the witness's credibility and character."
aspergere to splatter; to stain or defile: *a-* toward + *spargere* to scatter

disperse   **v.** to go or distribute in different directions, or over a wide area
"A Redcoat officer cried out to the militiamen: '<u>Disperse</u>, ye rebels!'"
dispergere to scatter widely: *dis-* down from + *spargere* to scatter

circumspect   **adj.** cautious or prudent; careful
"Patton was a bold, even rash general who found Montgomery too <u>circumspect</u>."
circumspicere to look around: *circum-* around + *spicere* to look at

despicable   **adj.** deserving hatred and contempt
"In wartime, a traitor is the most <u>despicable</u> of men."
despicari to scorn or disdain; to look down on: *de-* down + *spicere* to look at

introspective   **adj.** characterized by or given to self-reflection
"Prison affords inmates more than ample time for <u>introspection</u> and personal review."
introspicere to examine; to look into: *intro-* within; inside + *spicere* to look at

perspective   **n.** the art of representing three-dimensional objects on a two-dimensional surface so as to convey height, width, depth, and relative distance; a view or prospect; a point of view or way of looking at things

"A stereoscopic device creates realistic perspective from two photos."
perspicere to examine; to observe: *per-* through + *spicere* to look at

specimen   **n.** an individual animal, plant, or object used as an example of its species or type for scientific study or display; a sample for medical testing
"Audubon was a prolific hunter who painted hundreds of bird specimens."
specere to look at (variant of *spicere*)

spectacle   **n.** a visual striking performance or display
"Nero's Coliseum was an arena for spectacles such as gladiatorial contests and wild animals."
specere to look at

spectator   **n.** a member of the audience at a show, game, or other event; someone who watches, but does not participate in something
"At some soccer fields, players are protected from spectators by a moat."
specere to look at

specter   **n.** a ghost; an apparition
"Scrooge was moved to change his ways after encountering Marley's ghost and three other specters."
specere to look at

spectrum   **n.** a band of colors produced by separation of the components of light according to wavelength (as in a rainbow); a range
"The spectrum of European political opinion ranges from ultra-left to reactionary right."
specere to look at

aspire   **v.** to direct one's hopes or ambitions toward achieving something
"Hillary Clinton aspired to be the first woman president."
aspiration (n.)
aspirare to breathe; to influence: *ad-* toward + *spirare* to breathe

conspiracy   **n.** a secret plan by more than one person to do something harmful or unlawful
"Conspiracy theorists contend that Lee Oswald did not act alone when assassinating President Kennedy."
conspire (v.)
conspirare to agree; to plot: *con-* together with + *spirare* to breathe

dispirit   **v.** to cause to lose enthusiasm or hope
"Their team having lost, the dispirited fans quietly left the stadium."
dis- down from + *spirare* to breathe

expire   **v.** to come to the end of a period of validity; to die; to exhale
"The wounded Gaul collapsed and expired."
exspirare to breathe out; to die: *ex-* out + *spirare* to breathe

inspire   **v.** to fill with the urge to do or feel something; to animate someone; to inhale
"'The 1812 Overture' was inspired by Napoleon's defeat at Moscow."

	inspiration (n.) *inspirare* to breathe or blow into: *in-* in + *spirare* to breathe
respiratory	**adj.** relating to or affecting breathing "Leaves are the <u>respiratory</u> organs of plants, emitting oxygen and taking in carbon dioxide." *respirare* to breathe out: *re-* back, again + *spirare* to breathe
spirited	**adj.** full of energy, enthusiasm, and determination "Whirling dervishes perform a dizzying, <u>spirited</u> dance." *spirare* to breathe (the spirit of)
spiritual	**adj.** relating to or affecting the human spirit, as opposed to material or physical things; relating to religion or religious beliefs **n.** a religious song "A priest must tend to the <u>spiritual</u> needs of his parishioners." *spirare* to breathe (the spirit of)
transpire	**v.** to come to be known; to happen; (of a plant or leaf) to give off water vapor "It <u>transpired</u> that Phineas Fogg completed his balloon trip around the world in 80 days." *trans-* across; beyond + *spirare* to breathe

Exercise A

Fill in the blanks in the sentences below with the correct form of a word in the scroll above.

1. A _____ person chooses a new car carefully.

2. James Taylor's _____ performance delighted the audience.

3. The July Fourth fireworks display was a _____ that delighted young and old alike.

4. The warranty on my laptop computer will soon _____, so I need to get it fixed quickly.

5. Mathias _____ the seeds across the field, while his older brothers followed behind to till and water the soil.

6. Maybe if you offer your child a sweet snack for finishing his homework, it will _____ him to finish it more quickly.

7. The lake wasn't visible from the _____ of the ledge, but when he hiked higher up the mountain he got a clear view.

8. The crushing 0-18 defeat by the hated Hawks _____ the not-so-Mighty Ducks.

9. Every New England _____ at the Super Bowl began to cheer wildly when the Patriots came back and won.

10. John Kerry was furious at the _____ cast on his military record in Vietnam by the pro-Bush Swift Boat Veterans.

11. Al Quaida's _____ to crash a plane into the White House was foiled by passengers who sacrificed their lives to overwhelm the terrorist pilots.

12. The investigator was paid to find out exactly what had _____ on the day the victim died.

13. The nun's _____ nature served her well, as her convent enforced silence during meals.

14. During her years of piano lessons and devoted practice, she _____ to play at Carnegie Hall.

15. The _____ of Banquo haunted MacBeth.

16. Robbing children of their Christmas presents is _____.

17. Usually, a _____ infection like pneumonia cannot be cured without antibiotics.

18. After visiting the doctor, the patient stopped by the laboratory to have a blood _____ drawn for further tests.

19. We had a _____ experience that Easter morning, as we worshipped outside and the sun rose over the rustic cross and stone altar.

20. The visible light _____ encompasses seven base colors, ranging in wavelength from 400 nanometers (red) to 750 nanometers (violet).

Exercise B

Match the word with the letter of its definition.

1. ___ aspersion
2. ___ aspire
3. ___ circumspect
4. ___ conspiracy
5. ___ disperse
6. ___ dispirit
7. ___ despicable
8. ___ expire
9. ___ inspire
10. ___ introspective
11. ___ perspective
12. ___ respiratory
13. ___ specimen
14. ___ spectacle
15. ___ spectator
16. ___ specter
17. ___ spectrum
18. ___ spirited
19. ___ spiritual
20. ___ transpire

a) a ghost
b) full of energy, enthusiasm, and determination
c) an example of its species for scientific study
d) to fill with the urge to do something
e) relating to or affecting the lungs
f) to direct one's hopes towards achieving something
g) an attack on someone's character or reputation
h) the art of representing three-dimensional objects on a flat surface
i) to come to be known; to happen
j) deserving hatred and contempt
k) to cause to lose enthusiasm or hope
l) a band of colors, as in a rainbow
m) cautious or prudent
n) to distribute over a wide area
o) a visually striking performance or display
p) to reach the end of a period of validity
q) characterized by or given to introspection
r) a person who watches a show, game, or event
s) relating to the human spirit or religious beliefs
t) a secret plan by a group to do something harmful or unlawful

Exercise C

Solve the crossword puzzle.

Across
3. A band of colors produced by separation of the components of light according to wavelength (as in a rainbow); a range. 6. A person who watches a show, game, or other event. 8. To distribute in different directions or over a wide area. 9. The art of representing three-dimensional objects on a two-dimensional surface so as to convey height, width, depth, and relative distance; a view or prospect; a point of view. 12. An attack on someone's character or reputation. 13. Relating to or affecting the human spirit, as opposed to material or physical things; relating to religion or religious beliefs. 14. To fill with the urge or ability to do or feel something; to animate someone; to inhale. 15. A visually striking performance or display. 16. Deserving hatred and contempt. 17. To cause to loose enthusiasm or hope. 18. Cautious.

Down
1. Relating to or affecting respiration. 2. To come to be known; to happen; (of a plant or leaf) to give off water vapor. 3. An individual animal, plant, or object used as an example of its species or type for scientific study or display; a sample for medical testing. 4. A secret plan by a group to do something harmful or unlawful. 5. A ghost. 7. Characterized by or given to introspection. 10. To reach the end of the period of validity; to die; to exhale. 11. Full of energy, enthusiasm, and determination. 12. To direct one's hopes or ambitions toward achieving something.

Lesson XVIII
sta-/stit-, stella, string-, stru/struc-, suavis, sumere

STA-, STIT-
to stand

STELLA
star

STRING-
to bind

STRU-, STRUC-
to build

SUAVIS
sweet, agreeable

SUMERE
to take

constant, destitute, oust, restitution, constellation, stellar, astringent, constrain, constrict, strait, stringent, construct, construe, instruct, obstruct, assuage, suave, presume, subsume, sumptuous

Word Definitions

constant **adj.** occurring continuously
n. an unchanging situation or factor
"A lover is said to be '<u>constant</u>' if he or she remains faithful to the beloved."
constare to stand firm: *con-* with + *stare* to stand

destitute **adj.** extremely poor; lacking the means to provide for oneself
"The stock market collapse left many overextended investors <u>destitute</u>."
destitution (n.)
destitutus forsaken: *de-* down, from + *statutus* set in place; established

oust **v.** to drive out or expel from a position or place
"Fidel Castro and his band of rebels <u>ousted</u> the dictator Battista from power in Cuba."
obstare to oppose; to hinder: *ob-* against + *stare* to stand

restitution **n.** the restoration of something lost or stolen to its proper owner; recompense for injury or loss
"The judge ordered the vandal to pay $300 <u>restitution</u> to the car owner for breaking his windshield with a baseball bat."
restituere to restore: *re-* again + *statuere* to set in place; to establish

constellation	**n.** a group of stars forming a recognized pattern and typically named after a mythological figure; a pattern or web of relationships "Psychologists treat dysfunctions of the individual within the family <u>constellation</u>." *con-* with, together + *stella* star
stellar	**adj.** featuring or having the qualities of a star performer; relating to a star or stars "Nadia Comaneci put on a <u>stellar</u> balance beam performance." *stella* star
astringent	**adj.** causing the contraction of skin cells and other body tissues; sharp or severe in manner or style **n.** an astringent lotion applied to the skin for cosmetic purposes or to reduce bleeding from minor scrapes "Witch hazel is an <u>astringent</u> that can lessen wrinkles by drawing the skin taut." *astringere* to bind; to tighten: *a-* to (expressing intensity) + *stringere* to draw tight
constrain	**v.** to compel or force toward a course of action; to imprison "The rubberneckers were <u>constrained</u> by a police cordon around the accident scene." *constringere* to bind together tightly: *con-* with + *stringere* to draw tight
constrict	**v.** to make or become narrower, especially by encircling pressure "The girdle is no longer in vogue as a means to <u>constrict</u> the waistline." *constringere* to bind together tightly: *con-* with + *stringere* to draw tight
strait	**n.** a narrow passage of water connecting two seas or other large areas of water; a situation characterized by trouble or difficulty **adj.** narrow or cramped; strict or rigorous "To be 'between a rock and a hard place' is to be in dire <u>straits</u>." *stricta* drawn tight; narrow
stringent	**adj.** strict, precise, and exacting "<u>Stringent</u> regulations govern allowable vehicle emissions." *stringere* to draw tight
construct	**v.** to build or to erect; to form from various elements; to form according to grammatical rules **n.** an idea or theory; a group of words forming a phrase "He likes to <u>construct</u> theories; she likes to <u>construct</u> office buildings." *construere* to heap together; to build: *con-* together + *struere* to pile; to build
construe	**v.** to interpret in a particular way "White flags are typically <u>construed</u> as a sign of surrender." *construere* to heap together; to build: *con-* together + *struere* to pile; to build

instruct	v. to direct or command; to teach; to give information to "The commander <u>instructed</u> his aide to fetch maps of the terrain." *instruction (n.)* *instruere* to construct; to teach: *in-* in, upon + *struere* to pile; to build
obstruct	v. to be in the way of; to prevent or hinder "After a hurricane, downed trees frequently <u>obstruct</u> the roadways." *obstruction (n.)* *obstruere* to barricade: *ob-* against + *struere* to pile; to build
assuage	v. to make less intense, relieve, or decrease; to satisfy an appetite or desire "Reaching an oasis, the desert traveler finally <u>assuaged</u> his thirst." *ad-* to + *suavis* sweet; agreeable
suave	adj. charming, confident, and elegant "James Bond is portrayed as a <u>suave</u> man of elegant tastes." *suavis* sweet; agreeable
presume	v. to suppose that something is the case on the basis of probability "'Dr. Livingston, I <u>presume</u>?' were Stanley's words on first meeting the explorer." *presumption (n.)* *praesumere* to anticipate: *prae-* before + *sumere* to take up; to accept or select; to buy
subsume	v. to include or absorb into something else "The category 'biped' <u>subsumes</u> all two-footed creatures." *sub-* from below + *sumere* to take up; to accept or select; to buy
sumptuous	adj. splendid and expensive looking "An Arab sultan lives in <u>sumptuous</u>, palatial surroundings." *sumptus* costly (past participle of the verb *sumere* to buy)

Exercise A

Fill in the blanks in the sentences below with the correct form of a word in the scroll above.

1. The Thanksgiving feast is often the most _____ meal of the year.

2. It is incredibly dangerous to sail the Bering _____ without navigational equipment and a large, sturdy ship.

3. On a clear, moonless night, it can be very difficult to pick out an individual _____ from the bright Milky Way.

4. Therapy can sometimes help _____ the guilt of war veterans who have accidentally killed civilians during combat.

5. Since the ornate column tended to _____ their view of the stage, the spectators moved to better, empty theater seats.

6. Between the courthouse and the prison, the police had to _____ the convicts.

7. It takes many years of _____ training for Olympic athletes to win a medal.

8. Due to the school's _____ regulations, it was foolhardy to think that smoking or drinking would not lead to immediate expulsion.

9. The English professor tried to _____ the meaning of the poem with his students, but many in the class could not follow his line of thought.

10. Even though Bill Clinton was caught in a lie during the Monica Lewinsky scandal, he was not _____ from the presidency.

11. It is necessary to _____ the flow of money to terrorist organizations.

12. While he was _____ and sophisticated, she was crude and homely.

13. Russell Crowe's _____ performance in *Gladiator* won him an Oscar nomination.

14. Fredo asked the contractor to _____ his house within certain financial and time constraints.

15. Numerous charities collect money to aid _____ children in impoverished countries.

16. It is important to _____ children in good manners while they are young.

17. Her _____ comments put him off his game, ruffling his normal easy charm.

18. Jurors are supposed to _____ the innocence of the defendant, unless and until prosecutors prove him guilty beyond a reasonable doubt.

19. People injured on the job often receive some _____ in the form of Workers Compensation.

20. Scientists _____ monkeys, chimpanzees, and baboons into the category of primates.

Exercise B

Match the word with the letter of its definition.

1. ___ assuage
2. ___ astringent
3. ___ constant
4. ___ constellation
5. ___ constrain
6. ___ constrict
7. ___ construct
8. ___ construe
9. ___ destitute
10. ___ instruct
11. ___ obstruct
12. ___ oust
13. ___ presume
14. ___ restitution
15. ___ stellar
16. ___ strait
17. ___ stringent
18. ___ suave
19. ___ subsume
20. ___ sumptuous

a) recompense for injury or loss
b) to interpret in a particular way
c) a narrow passage of water connecting two seas
d) to make or become narrower
e) charming, confident, and elegant
f) to include or absorb in something else
g) to be in the way of; to prevent or hinder
h) a group of stars forming a recognized pattern
i) to make less intense, relieve, or decrease; to satisfy a desire or appetite
j) splendid and expensive
k) to suppose that something is the case
l) to give information to; to teach
m) a lotion that is applied to the skin to tighten the pores
n) lacking the means to provide for oneself
o) to compel or force toward a course of action
p) occurring continuously
q) strict, precise, and exacting
r) to build or erect
s) featuring the qualities of a star performer
t) to drive out or expel from a position or place

Exercise C

Solve the crossword puzzle.

Across

2 Charming, confident, and elegant **3** To drive out or expel from a position or place **5** Splendid and expensive looking **8** Strict, precise, and exacting **10** To direct or command; to teach; to give information to **12** Sharp or severe in manner or style **13** An unchanging situation or factor **16** To be in the way of; to prevent or hinder **17** A group of stars named after a mythological figure **18** To suppose that something is the case on the basis of probability

Down

1 To include or absorb into something else **2** A narrow passage of water connecting two seas **4** To make narrower, especially by encircling pressure **6** To compel or force toward a course of action **7** Extremely poor; lacking the means to provide for oneself **9** The restoration of something lost or stolen to its proper owner **11** To build or to erect; to form from various elements **13** To interpret in a particular way **14** To make less intense, relieve, or decrease **15** Relating to a star or stars

Lesson XIX
tact-/tang-/ting-, temere, temper-, tempore

TACT, TANG, TING
to touch

TEMPER-
to combine

TEMERE
rashly, blindly

TEMPORE
time

> *contiguous, contingent, intangible, tact, tactile, tangent, tangible,*
> *temerarious, temerity*
> *temper, temperament, temperance, temperate, tempered,*
> *contemporary, extemporaneous, tempest, tempo, temporal, temporize*

Word Definitions

contiguous
adj. sharing an edge or boundary; adjacent; connected in time or space without a break
"The former East and West Germany, once contiguous communist and capitalist nations, are now a single country."
contingere to connect with; to affect: *con-* together + *tangere* to touch

contingent
adj. liable to occur, but not certain; dependent on conditions or occurrences not yet established
"Attending the concert is contingent on procuring tickets."
contingency (n.)
contingere to connect with; to affect: *con-* together + *tangere* to touch

intangible
adj. incapable of being perceived by the senses; incapable of being precisely defined or predicted
"A timely arrival depends on weather, unforeseen delays, traffic, and other intangibles."
in- not + *tangere* to touch

tact
n. acute sensitivity to what is proper and appropriate when dealing with others, including the ability to speak or act without offending
"A diplomat must use tact in discussing controversial political issues."
tactus touch

125

tactile	**adj.** perceptible to the sense of touch; relating to or proceeding from the sense of touch "The silk was plain in appearance, but its <u>tactile</u> properties were sumptuous." *tangere* to touch
tangent	**n.** a straight line or plane that touches a curve or surface at a point or along a single line; an irrelevant line of thought or conversation **adj.** touching but not intersecting "To 'go off on a <u>tangent</u>' is to digress from the topic at hand." *tangere* to touch
tangible	**adj.** discernible by touch; palpable; possible to touch; possible to treat as fact; possible to understand or realize "In legal terminology, 'material evidence' refers to <u>tangible</u> clues." *tangere* to touch
temerarious	**adj.** rash; recklessly daring "Evel Knievel's death-defying motorcycle stunts evinced a <u>temerarious</u> character." *temere* rashly; blindly
temerity	**n.** foolhardy disregard of danger; excessive confidence or boldness "The unwanted guests had the <u>temerity</u> to crash the party." *temeritas* rashness
temper	**n.** a person's state of mind or emotions; composure; a tendency to become easily angry or irritable; an outbreak of rage **v.** to moderate; to bring to a desired consistency, texture or hardness; to harden or strengthen by heating, or by heating and cooling; to strengthen through experience or hardship; to toughen "His enthusiasm for shark fishing was <u>tempered</u> by an appreciation of its dangers." *temperare* to blend; to refrain from
temperament	**n.** an individual's manner of thinking, behaving, and reacting; demeanor and comportment; excessive irritability or sensitivity "Her <u>temperament</u> was very mild, but her husband was irritable and hot-tempered." *temperare* to blend; to refrain from
temperance	**n.** moderation and self-restraint in behavior; restraint in the use of, or abstinence from, alcoholic beverages. "Carry Nation took her axe to saloon beer barrels in her <u>temperance</u> crusade." *temperare* to blend; to refrain from
temperate	**adj.** moderate in conduct and speech; moderate in degree or quality; marked by moderate temperatures, weather, or climate; neither hot nor cold "<u>Temperate</u> climates are best suited to agriculture." *temperatus* mild

tempered	**adj.** having a specific temper or disposition; made hard or flexible by tempering; having the requisite degree of hardness or elasticity "A sword is <u>tempered</u> by repeated heating, hammering, folding, and reheating." *temperare* to blend; to refrain from
contemporary	**adj.** belonging to the same period of time as something or someone else; about the same age; current or modern **n.** a person of about the same age or generation "The Metropolitan Museum features both historical and <u>contemporary</u> art." *contemporarius* contemporary: *con-* with + *tempore* time; condition
extemporaneous	**adj.** carried out or performed with little or no preparation; impromptu; prepared in advance but delivered without notes or text "The candidate, who usually followed a well-vetted script, spoke <u>extemporaneously</u> at the Town Hall." *ex tempore*: *ex-* from; out + *tempore* time; condition
tempest	**n.** a violent windstorm, frequently accompanied by rain, snow, or hail; furious agitation, commotion, or tumult; an uproar "'A <u>tempest</u> in a teapot' means a lot of fuss about a trivial matter." *temporis, tempus* time; condition; season
tempo	**n.** the speed at which music is or ought to be played; a characteristic rate or rhythm of activity "Some conductors prefer a quicker <u>tempo</u> for this movement, but I prefer a more measured pace." *tempore* time
temporal	**adj.** limited by time; worldly, not eternal; secular or lay; of or relating to the temple (of the skull) "According to Christian adherents, <u>temporal</u> life is followed by an eternal one." *tempus, temporis* time; condition; season *templum, templi* temple
temporize	**v.** to act evasively to gain time, avoid argument, or postpone a decision; to engage in discussions to achieve a compromise or gain time "When his fiancee asked him to set a date for the wedding, Jim, who was getting cold feet, <u>temporized</u>." *temporizare* to pass the time < *temporis, tempus* time; season

Exercise A

Fill in the blanks in the sentences below with the correct form of a word in the scroll above.

1. In the grand scheme of time, humans lead a fleeting, _____ existence.

2. Before the _____ movement, there were no restrictions on the sales of alcoholic beverages.

3. Katharine's father and John's mother were _____; both had lived through the privations of the Great Depression and the anxieties and loss of World War II.

4. The college scholarship was _____ on her graduation from high school with a grade point average of 3.5 or higher.

5. The firefighter's even _____ was especially helpful in keeping people calm during emergencies.

6. The _____ swept across the island, leaving roofless shanties and downed trees in its wake.

7. As soon as she found _____ evidence of a break-in, she called police.

8. In the United States, there are forty-eight _____ states, plus Alaska and Hawaii, which don't share any borders with the "lower 48;" the District of Columbia; and several island territories.

9. Stand-up comedians who improvise their routines rely on quick thinking for their _____ delivery.

10. The touch tank at the aquarium offered a _____ experience for the children.

11. The band's performance sounded unpolished because the trumpet player had not practiced and could not keep _____ with the other musicians.

12. Many teenagers act with reckless _____ when they secretly smoke marijuana and imbibe large quantities of alcohol.

13. The president relied on the secretary of state's _____ to handle a very touchy situation.

14. Most people prefer a more _____ climate to one that is extremely hot or cold.

15. Displays of outrage and _____ may be an indication of a more serious psychological problem.

16. Mr. Beaven, when discussing vocabulary words with his students, often heads off on random _____ unrelated to their studies.

17. The most difficult things to place a dollar value on, when assessing a business before dividing or selling it, are _____ such as "good will – the business's reputation and client confidence.

18. The salesman explained that the _____ steel product was of higher quality and therefore was more expensive.

19. Jeffrey's _____ behavior sometimes got him in trouble.

20. The daughter offered lengthy excuses to _____ when her mother demanded she clean up her room.

Exercise B

Match the word with the letter of its definition.

1. contemporary
2. contiguous
3. contingent
4. extemporaneous
5. intangible
6. tact
7. tactile
8. tangent
9. tangible
10. temerarious
11. temerity
12. temper
13. temperance
14. temperate
15. temperament
16. tempered
17. tempest
18. tempo
19. temporal
20. temporize

a) impromptu
b) perceptible to the sense of touch
c) possible to touch or to treat as fact
d) foolhardy disregard of danger
e) moderation and self-restraint
f) having the requisite degree of hardness
g) belonging to the same period of time
h) the speed at which music is played
i) the ability to speak or act without offending
j) touching but not intersecting; an irrelevant topic
k) limited by time; not eternal
l) to act evasively to gain time
m) sharing an edge or boundary
n) a violent wind storm
o) presumptuously or recklessly daring
p) conditional
q) moderate in degree or quality
r) incapable of being touched; unquantifiable
s) a person's state of mind or emotions; an angry outburst
t) a person's disposition and demeanor

Exercise C

Solve the crossword puzzle.

Across
1. Having a specific temper or disposition; hardened by heat. 3. Sharing an edge or boundary. 4. Excessive irritability or sensitivity. 6. Lasting only for a time. 7. Dependent on conditions or occurrences not yet established; conditional. 9. Incapable of being perceived by the senses; incapable of being precisely defined or predicted. 10. Discernible by touch, palpable; possible to treat as fact; possible to understand or realize. 12. A violent windstorm, frequently accompanied by rain, snow, or hail; furious agitation, commotion, or tumult; an uproar. 14. Presumptuously or recklessly daring. 16. Perceptible to the sense of touch; relating to or proceeding from the sense of touch. 17. A straight line or plane that touches a curve or surface at one point or along a single line; an irrelevant line of speech. 18. Foolhardy disregard of danger; excessive confidence or boldness.

Down
2. Carried out or performed with little or n preparation; impromptu; prepared in advance but delivered without notes or text. 5. Belonging to the same period of time; current. 8. A person's disposition and demeanor; composure; a tendency to become easily angry or irritable; an outbreak of rage. 10. The speed at which music is or ought to be played; a characteristic rate or rhythm of activity. 11. Moderation and self-restraint; moderate in degree or quality; marked by moderate temperatures, weather, or climate; neither hot nor cold. 13. To act evasively to gain time, avoid argument, or postpone a decision; to engage in discussions to achieve a compromise or gain time. 14. Moderation and self-restraint in behavior; restraint in the use of, or abstinence from, alcoholic beverages. 15. Acute sensitivity to what is proper and appropriate when dealing with others, including the ability to speak or act without offending.

Lesson XX
-tain/ten-/tin-, term-, terra

-TAIN, TEN-, TIN-
to hold

TERM-
end

TERRA
land, earth

contain, detain, impertinent, pertain, pertinacious, pertinent, retain, retentive, tenable, tenacious, tenure, interminable, terminate, extraterrestrial, inter, mediterranean, subterranean, terracotta, terrain, terrestrial

Word Definitions

contain
v. to have within or to be capable of holding; to keep within limits; to restrain; to halt the spread or development of; to check the expansion or influence of
"A quarantine <u>contained</u> the hoof-and-mouth outbreak to one rural county."
continere to hold in position: *con-* together + *tenere* to hold

detain
v. to keep from proceeding; to delay or slow; to keep in police or military custody or temporary confinement
"The drunken driving suspect was <u>detained</u> overnight and released in the morning."
detinere to hold off; to take prisoner: *de-* down, from + *tenere* to hold

impertinent
adj. exceeding the limits of propriety or good manners; improperly forward
"Interrupting a speaker is considered <u>impertinent</u>."
im- not + *pertinere* to pertain to: *per-* through, by + *tenere* to hold

pertain
v. to refer; to relate; to belong as an adjunct part, holding or quality
"Rules and laws do not <u>pertain</u> to a despot with absolute power."
pertinere to pertain to: *per-* through, by + *tenere* to hold

pertinacious
adj. holding tenaciously to a purpose, belief, opinion, or course of action; stubbornly or perversely persistent; obstinate
"She was <u>pertinacious</u> in her lobbying efforts, despite the senator's well-known opposition to her position."
pertinere to pertain to: *per-* through, by + *tenere* to hold

pertinent	**adj.** logically relevant to the subject matter "A court permits only evidence <u>pertinent</u> to the guilt or innocence of the accused." *pertinere* to pertain to: *per-* through, by + *tenere* to hold
retain	**v.** to keep possession of; to keep or hold in a particular place, condition or position; to keep in mind; to remember; to hire by paying a fee "Some feminists opt to <u>retain</u> their maiden names after marriage." *retinere* to preserve; to restrain: *re-* back, again + *tenere* to hold
retentive	**adj.** having the quality, power, or capacity to retain; having the ability to retain information or knowledge with ease "A photographic mind is highly <u>retentive</u> of visual information." *retinere* to preserve; to restrain: *re-* back, again + *tenere* to hold
tenable	**adj.** (of a position or theory) rationally defensible; able to withstand assault "Fort Sumter proved <u>untenable</u> and was surrendered to the Confederate bombardiers." *tenere* to hold; to possess; to preserve
tenacious	**adj.** holding or clinging fast (to an object, person, or idea); persistent; steadfast "Rock climbers need a <u>tenacious</u> grip." *tenacity (n.)* *tenax, tenacis* clinging; stubborn; persistent < *tenere* to hold
tenure	**n.** the act, fact, or condition of holding something in one's possession; a period during which something is held; a job guarantee until retirement "Franklin Roosevelt had the longest <u>tenure</u> of any president." *tenere* to hold
interminable	**adj.** being or seeming to be endless; continual; tiresomely long; wearisome "Fidel Castro's seemingly <u>interminable</u> speeches last five hours or more." *interminatus* endless: *in-* not + *terminatus* concluded; restricted; ended
terminate	**v.** to bring to an end or to halt; to occur at or form the end of; to conclude or finish; to fire someone from a job; to kill (slang) "The insubordinate worker was promptly <u>terminated</u>." *termination (n.)* *terminus* end
extraterrestrial	**adj.** originating, located, or occurring outside Earth or its atmosphere **n.** an extraterrestrial life form "Meteors are <u>extraterrestrial</u> objects that usually burn up in earth's atmosphere." *extra-* beyond, outside + *terrestris* of the earth < *terra* earth
inter	**v.** to place in a grave or tomb; to bury "Only those who have performed military service may be <u>interred</u> in Arlington National Cemetery." *interrare* within the earth: *in-* in + *terra* earth; land

mediterranean	**adj.**	surrounded nearly or completely by dry land
		"The Caspian Sea is in fact a <u>mediterranean</u> lake."
		mediterraneus inland: *media* in the middle of + *terra* earth; land
subterranean	**adj.**	situated or operating beneath the earth's surface; underground; hidden; secret
		"The gold sarcophagus of Tutankhamen was discovered in a <u>subterranean</u> tomb."
		subterraneus underground: *sub-* under + *terra* earth; land
terracotta	**n.**	a hard ceramic clay used in pottery and building construction, often brownish-orange in color; ceramic wares made of this material
	adj.	brownish-orange
		"<u>Terracotta</u> tiles are used extensively in Italian roofs."
		terra earth + *cocta* cooked
terrain	**n.**	an area of land; a particular geographic area or region; the surface features or topography of a particular area of land
		"The <u>terrain</u> was hilly and dotted with rocks and boulders."
		terrenus, terrena of earth; earthy
terrestrial	**adj.**	of or relating to the earth or its inhabitants; having a worldly, mundane character or quality; of, relating to, or composed of land
		"While turtles may be aquatic or amphibious, tortoises are <u>terrestrial</u> only."
		terrestris of the earth < *terra* earth

Exercise A

Fill in the blanks in the sentences below with the correct form of a word in the scroll above.

1. He was finally promoted to professor and awarded _____ shortly after his fortieth birthday.

2. Phoenicia, Carthage, Greece, Sicily, and Rome dominated the region surrounding the _____ Sea in ancient times.

3. Michael Jackson will be _____ until a judge can arraign him and set bail.

4. The valedictorian attributed her excellent grades to her family's support, her own motivation, and her _____ memory.

5. _____ animals have quite different characteristics than aquatic ones.

6. After living in the mountains most of his life, the skier was quite familiar with the _____ .

7. After a nearly _____ journey across the ocean, the Pilgrims finally sighted land.

8. He built a puzzle box to _____ his treasure map, a rare coin, and a few antique jewels.

9. They could no longer afford to _____ the land that had been in their family for nearly 300 years.

10. It was a cold, rainy day in late March when the ground had thawed and it was time to _____ those who had died during the winter.

11. Despite his mounting debts, Tom clung to a _____ belief that God would help him find a way to save his house from foreclosure.

12. The old woman's _____ hold on life never ceased to amaze her doctors, even while it disappointed her inheritors.

13. That tangent doesn't _____ to the subject of the book, slows the storyline, and should be cut.

14. Your strictly behaviorist theory about group behavior is _____, but doesn't appear to account for phenomena such as altruism and self-sacrifice.

15. The Viet Cong used _____ tunnels to get behind enemy lines and kill patrolling U.S. and South Vietnamese soldiers.

16. The city council wished to _____ the public hearing after two hours, but more speakers kept lining up behind the microphone.

17. His father repeatedly chastised him for his _____ remarks.

18. We might have completed the interview in half the time, if only we had been able to stick to _____ subjects.

19. Those who believed in benevolent _____ beings chased after the UFO in their cars or on foot, hoping to witness a landing.

20. The ancient _____ tiles had to be lifted one by one from the archaeological site.

Exercise B

Match the word with the letter of its definition.

1. ___ contain
2. ___ detain
3. ___ extraterrestrial
4. ___ impertinent
5. ___ inter
6. ___ interminable
7. ___ Mediterranean
8. ___ pertain
9. ___ pertinacious
10. ___ pertinent
11. ___ retain
12. ___ retentive
13. ___ subterranean
14. ___ tenable
15. ___ tenacious
16. ___ tenure
17. ___ terracotta
18. ___ terrain
19. ___ terminate
20. ___ terrestrial

a) a period during which something is held; job security
b) relevant to the matter at hand
c) to refer; to relate
d) originating or occurring outside Earth
e) an area of land or its surface features
f) to hold or keep within limits
g) having the quality, power, or capacity to retain
h) to keep possession of
i) beneath the surface (of the earth)
j) holding persistently to something
k) to end
l) being or seeming to be endless
m) to delay or slow; to confine (in jail or police custody)
n) improperly forward or bold
o) holding tenaciously to a purpose, belief, or course of action
p) to place in a grave or tomb
q) surrounded or nearly surrounded by land
r) relating to the earth or its inhabitants
s) rationally defensible; able to withstand assault
t) hardened clay used in pottery and building construction

Exercise C

Solve the crossword puzzle.

Across
2. To refer or relate; to belong as an adjunct part or quality. 4. Persistent; steadfast. 6. A clay, usually reddish-brown, used in pottery and building construction. 7. Having precise logical relevance to the matter at hand. 11. Having the quality, power, or capacity to retain. 14. Surrounded nearly or completely by land. 15. To place in a grave or tomb. 16. To hold within; to prevent from spreading. 17. Capable of being upheld in argument. 18. Holding tenaciously to a purpose, belief, opinion, or course of action. 19. Of or relating to the earth or its inhabitants. 20. Being or seeming to be endless.

Down
1. To prevent from proceeding; to take into custody. 3. An area of land. 5. Underground. 8. An extraterrestrial life form. 9. To keep. 10. To bring to an end or halt. 12. Improperly forward or impolite. 13. The act, fact, or condition of holding something in one's possession; length of service (in a job or position).

Test 3

Choose the correct meaning for the underlined vocabulary word in each sentence.

1. "Lupton's broad face might well wear a smile of complacency as she contemplated the heir of Hunsden Wood occupied in paying <u>assiduous</u> court to her darling Sarah Martha."

    The Professor by Charlotte Bronte

    (a) lecherous (b) flowery (c) showing great care (d) unprompted
    (e) stringent

2. "Here the class was reciting a lesson from an abstruse textbook on economics, reciting it by rote, with so obvious a failure to <u>assimilate</u> it that the waste of labour was pitiful."

    Up From Slavery by Booker T. Washington

    (a) absorb (b) feel bitterness (c) imitate (d) clarify
    (e) memorize

3. "Happiness consumes itself like a flame. It cannot burn forever, it must go out, and the <u>presentiment</u> of its end destroys it at its very peak."

    A Dream Play by August Strindberg

    (a) agreement (b) premonition (c) view, opinion
    (d) expression of approval (e) emotion

4. "At times he would tear off a small piece, and holding it between his paws, and retaining his <u>sedentary</u> position, would feed himself with it, after the fashion of a monkey."

    The Adventures of Captain Bonneville by Washington Irving

    (a) calm (b) hanging (c) awkward (d) sitting (e) standing

5. "He had never before seen a woman's lips and teeth which forced upon his mind with such persistent iteration the old Elizabethan <u>simile</u> of roses filled with snow."

    Tess of the d'Urbervilles by Thomas Hardy

    (a) bouquet (b) figure of speech (c) imitation (d) similarity (e) appearance

6. "'Well, sir,' answered Benjamin, 'I am that Partridge; but I here absolve you from all filial duty, for I do assure you, you are no son of mine.'"
   The History of Tom Jones, a Foundling by Henry Fielding

   (a) stop   (b) require   (c) free   (d) incorporate   (e) prevent

7. "Not only did his contemporaries, carried away by their passions, talk in this way, but posterity and history have acclaimed Napoleon as grand, while Kutuzov is described by foreigners as a crafty, dissolute, weak old courtier, and by Russians as something indefinite – a sort of puppet useful only because he had a Russian name."
   War and Peace by Leo Tolstoy

   (a) warm and happy   (b) diminished   (c) imaginative
   (d) unrestrained, debauched   (e) firm, ripe

8. "For the first time Martin's glorious sleep was interrupted by insomnia, and he tossed through long, restless nights."
   Martin Eden by Jack London

   (a) sleeplessness   (b) drowsiness   (c) medication   (d) speed
   (e) restfulness

9. "He interrupted his earnest mental soliloquy with a jocular thought at his own expense."
   Under Western Eyes by Joseph Conrad

   (a) belief that only the self exists   (b) performance of several people
   (c) monologue   (d) valued principle   (e) loneliness

10. "At this moment she tossed her head in unison with her thoughts, when down fell the milk pail to the ground, and all her imaginary schemes perished in a moment."
    Fables by Aesop

    (a) great sympathy   (b) continuing sound   (c) minor component
    (d) dissolving an image   (e) at the same time

11. "He did not like that text; it seemed to cast an aspersion on himself."
    Of Human Bondage by W. Somerset Maugham

    (a) distress   (b) prudence   (c) self-reflection   (d) insult   (e) doubt

12. "However, nothing dispirits, and nothing seems worthwhile disputing."
    Moby Dick by Herman Melville

    (a) exhales   (b) discourages   (c) dies   (d) animates   (e) inhales

13. "These closely similar particulars are collected together by their similarity primarily and, more correctly, by the fact that they are related to each other approximately according to the laws of <u>perspective</u> and of reflection and diffraction of light."
The Analysis of Mind by Bertrand Russell

    (a) point of view   (b) wavelength   (c) spectrum   (d) secret plan
    (e) band of colors

14. "At each end of the solar <u>spectrum</u> the chemist can detect the presence of what are known as 'actinic' rays."
Can Such Things Be? by Ambrose Bierce

    (a) apparition   (b) aurora   (c) range of light values
    (d) flares and storms   (e) chemical reaction

15. "Do, messieurs, do all that your hearts counsel you to <u>assuage</u> the grief of Madame Fouquet."
The Man in the Iron Mask by Alexandre Dumas

    (a) suppose   (b) decrease   (c) interpret   (d) prevent   (e) interrupt

16. "Instead of keeping close to me and trying to <u>oust</u> me from the slit, the curate had gone back into the scullery."
The War Of The Worlds by H.G. Wells

    (a) imprison   (b) compel   (c) erect   (d) eject   (e) command

17. "In the course of his lark he managed to make a wide breach in one of the university's most <u>stringent</u> laws."
A Tramp Abroad by Mark Twain

    (a) elegant   (b) rigorous   (c) cramped   (d) sharp   (e) eloquent

18. "Porthos lived in an apartment, large in size and of very <u>sumptuous</u> appearance, in the Rue du Vieux-Colombier."
The Three Musketeers by Alexandre Dumas

    (a) charming   (b) confident   (c) strict   (d) lavish   (e) stylish

19. "I felt myself being pushed into a little room <u>contiguous</u> to the wardrobe room."
20,000 Leagues Under The Sea by Jules Verne

    (a) conditional   (b) intangible   (c) adjacent   (d) tactual   (e) palpable

20. "The child, sitting down with the old man close behind it, had been thinking how

strange it was that horses who were such fine honest creatures should seem to make vagabonds of all the men they drew about them, when a loud laugh at some extemporaneous witticism of Mr. Short's, having allusion to the circumstances of the day, roused her from her meditation and caused her to look around."

The Old Curiosity Shop by Charles Dickens

(a) current, modern   (b) impromptu   (c) brief   (d) moderate   (e) daring

21. "The things which are seen are temporal; but the things which are not seen are eternal."

The Bible, II Corinthians, 4:18

(a) rhythmic   (b) sacred   (c) modern   (d) earthly   (e) restrained

22. "I like him on the whole very well; he is clever and has a good deal to say, but he is sometimes impertinent and troublesome."

Lady Susan by Jane Austen

(a) impolite   (b) annoying   (c) wearisome   (d) defensible   (e) tireless

23. "After a time that seemed interminable, they emerged from the circling wood."

The Lair of the White Worm by Bram Stoker

(a) surprisingly quick   (b) endless   (c) cohesive   (d) worldly   (e) improperly forward

24. "So far indeed did his information extend, and so acutely retentive was his memory, that he was supposed to be the only man who could have told you who Julius Beaufort, the banker, really was, and what had become of handsome Bob Spicer."

The Age of Innocence by Edith Wharton

(a) bringing to a halt   (b) logical   (c) able to hold   (d) possessive   (e) clear and cohesive

25. "To become a token woman – whether you win the Nobel Prize or merely get tenure at the cost of denying your sisters – is to become something less than a man ... since men are loyal at least to their own world-view, their laws of brotherhood and self-interest."

Ms. Magazine, Adrienne Rich

(a) job security   (b) area   (c) exclusive use   (d) region   (e) tomb or grave

Lesson XXI

textus, torq-/tors-/tort-, totus, tract-, trud-/trus-, turbare

TEXTUS
woven

TORQ-, TORS-, TORT-
to twist

TOTUS
all, entire

TRACT-
to drag

TRUD-, TRUS-
to push, shove

TURBARE
to disturb

> *context, pretext, contort, distort, retort, torque, torsion, tortuous, totalitarian, detract, distract, extract, intractable, abstruse, extrude, intrude, obtrude, protrude, imperturbable, turbid*

Word Definitions

context
n. the part of a text or statement that surrounds a particular word or passage and determines its meaning; the setting (for an event)
"All is fair in the context of romance or war."
contextual (adj.), contextualize (v.)
contextus connected (past participle of the verb *contexere* to connect: *con-* together + *texere* to weave)

pretext
n. an ostensible or professed purpose; an excuse; an effort or strategy intended to conceal something
"The pretext for the war was to bring democracy to the Middle East; the real reason was control of oil."
preatextus cloaked (past participle of the verb *preatexere* to cloak; to pretend: *prae-* before + *texere* to weave)

contort
v. to twist, wrench, or bend severely out of shape; to become twisted into a strained shape or expression
"A pretzel is a contorted piece of dough that is baked and salted."
contortion (n.), contortionist (n.)
contortus twisted or crooked (past participle of the verb *contorquere*: *con-* together + *torquere* to twist)

distort
v. to twist out of a proper or natural relation of parts; to misshape; to give a false or misleading account of; to misrepresent; to pervert
"The claim that slavery alone led to the Civil War distorts a more complex truth."
distortion (n.)

distortus misshapen (past participle of the verb *distorquere*: *dis-* down from, apart + *torquere* to twist)

retort
v. to reply or answer in a quick, caustic, or witty manner; to present a counter-argument; to retaliate; to return in kind
n. a quick incisive reply; the act or instance of retorting
"After the Normandy invasion, Hitler <u>retorted</u> with a December counterattack."
retortus twisted back (past participle of the verb *retorquere* to twist or cast back: *re-* back, again + *torquere* to twist)

torque
n. the measure of a force's tendency to produce torsion and rotation about an axis, against resistance; a turning or twisting force
"A screwdriver relies on <u>torque</u> to drive home a screw."
torquere to twist

torsion
n. the act or force of twisting or turning; the condition of being twisted or turned; the stress or deformation caused when one end of an object is twisted in one direction and the other is motionless or twisted oppositely
"<u>Torsion</u> applied to the axles propels a wheeled vehicle."
torsi (simple past of *torquere* to twist)

tortuous
adj. winding or twisting (of a path, journey, etc.); circuitous or devious (of an explanation or series of related events); highly complex (of a task)
"With its twisting body, a snake traces a <u>tortuous</u> path as it slithers forward."
tortus twisted (past participle of the verb *torquere* to twist)

totalitarian
adj. a form of government in which the political authority exercises absolute and centralized control over all aspects of life
"Plato's *Republic* describes a <u>totalitarian</u> regime headed by a despotic philosopher king."
totus, tota all; entire; total

detract
v. to draw or take away from; to divert; to reduce the value, importance, or quality of
"The offshore wind farm <u>detracted</u> from the ocean view."
detractus excluded; omitted (past participle of the verb *detrahere* to drag away; to exclude: *de-* away + *trahere* to drag; to draw)

distract
v. to pull away from the original or desired object of attention or interest; to divert; to pull in another emotional direction; to unsettle
"Video games <u>distract</u> some teens for hours each day and compromise homework time."
distraction (n.)
distractus distracted (past participle of *distrahere*: *dis-* apart + *trahere* to draw or drag)

extract
v. to derive or obtain from a source; to obtain despite resistance; to excerpt or summarize (from a text); to deduce; to learn from an experience
n. an excerpt or summary; a concentrated essence of something

"Aspirin is an <u>extract</u> of willow tree bark."
extraction (n.)
extractus drawn out (past participle of *extrahere*: *ex-* out- + *trahere* to draw or drag)

intractable　　**adj.** difficult to manage or govern; stubborn; unruly; difficult to mold or manipulate; difficult to alleviate, remedy, or cure
"For many would-be puzzle solvers, Rubik's Cube has proved <u>intractable</u>."
in- not + *tractus* drawn out

abstruse　　**adj.** difficult to understand; recondite; obscure
"The medieval alchemy text contains <u>abstruse</u> formulas and mysterious symbols."
abstrudere to hide or conceal: *abs-*, *ab-* from + *trudere* to push; to shove

extrude　　**v.** to push or thrust out; to shape by forcing through a die
"Liquid nylon is <u>extruded</u> through tiny holes and dried to produce fibers."
extrudere to push out: *ex-* out- + *trudere* to push; to shove

intrude　　**v.** to put or force in inappropriately, especially without invitation, fitness, or permission; to enter as an improper or unwanted element
"Loud street noises <u>intruded</u> on the reader's concentration."
intrusion (n.)
intrudere to push in: *in-* into + *trudere* to push; to shove

obtrude　　**v.** to impose one's self on others with undue insistence or without invitation; to thrust out
"Protesters <u>obtruded</u> into the meeting hall to disrupt the proceedings."
obtrudere to obtrude: *ob-* against + *trudere* to push; to shove

protrude　　**v.** to push forward; to jut out; to project
"A parti-colored handkerchief <u>protruded</u> from the dandy's vest pocket."
protrusion (n.)
protrudere to thrust forward: *pro-* before + *trudere* to push; to thrust

imperturbable　　**adj.** unshakably calm and collected; unable to be upset or excited
"The Buddha is portrayed in statuary as an <u>imperturbable</u>, meditative figure"
im- not + *perturbare* to confuse or disturb: *per-* through + *turbare* to disturb or agitate

turbid　　**adj.** muddy or full of sediment; heavy, dark, or dense (smoke or fog); in a state of turmoil; muddled
"The motorboat left a <u>turbid</u> wake in the shallow pond."
turbidus disordered (past participle of *turbare* to disturb or agitate)

Exercise A

Fill in the blanks in the sentences below with the correct form of a word in the scroll above.

1. The orthodontist showed the patient how his _____ front teeth could be aligned with braces.

2. He liked to _____ his big brother from his homework and get him to wrestly.

3. He tried not to _____ his opinions, but was unable to help himself when he overheard someone repeating a campaign smear as if it were truthful.

4. Houdini's amazing escape and disappearance acts were dependent on his ability to _____ his body.

5. The author wrote in an _____ style, making the text difficult to fathom.

6. The heavy-duty _____ bar on the car was part of the special suspension system that came with the sports package.

7. During the first few days of his imprisonment, we were not able to _____ any helpful information from the captured spy.

8. Because all the boat traffic in the canal had made the water _____, we could not find her glasses after they fell overboard.

9. The overgrown shrubs in front of the house _____ from its curb appeal.

10. If you are not sure of a word's meaning, you can often determine it from the _____ of the passage.

11. Jim _____ spaghetti through the small round holes in his pasta machine.

12. The highway along the Riviera, although scenic, has many _____ curves.

13. They surrounded us using the _____ of a friendly rescue, when in fact they wanted to capture us.

14. It was like watching a verbal tennis match: First one would make a comment and then the other would _____ with lightening speed.

15. Even in the midst of the riot, the police remained _____.

16. The teacher asked in class today if anyone could name a country with a _____ form of government.

17. I can't stand listening to Bill O'Reilly because he's so unfair when confronting ordinary talk show guests: He always _____ what they say.

18. She tried locking the door so no one could _____ on her privacy.

19. The doctor prescribed moderate doses of narcotics to give the dying patient some relief from the _____ pain.

20. What you need to loosen that bolt is a bigger wrench, because the longer handle will give you better leverage and _____.

Exercise B

Match the word with the letter of its definition.

1. ___ abstruse
2. ___ context
3. ___ contort
4. ___ detract
5. ___ distort
6. ___ distract
7. ___ extract
8. ___ extrude
9. ___ imperturbable
10. ___ intractable
11. ___ intrude
12. ___ obtrude
13. ___ pretext
14. ___ protrude
15. ___ retort
16. ___ torque
17. ___ torsion
18. ___ tortuous
19. ___ totalitarian
20. ___ turbid

a) an excuse
b) a force that tends to cause rotation
c) to impose on someone
d) unshakably calm and collected
e) to thrust or force out
f) winding, twisting, or highly complex
g) to put or force in inappropriately
h) to reply in a quick, caustic, or witty manner
i) to misshape or misrepresent
j) cloudy or opaque; muddled
k) to remove from a source despite resistance
l) (of a government) exercising absolute control
m) to reduce the value, importance, or quality of
n) the act of twisting or turning
o) to jut out; to project
p) difficult to understand
q) to twist or bend out of shape
r) difficult to control or deal with; stubborn
s) to pull someone's attention in a different direction
t) the circumstances that form the setting for an event, statement, or idea

Exercise C

Solve the crossword puzzle:

Across

1. To put or force in inappropriately. 3. To reply or to answer in a quick, caustic, or witty manner. 5. To draw or pull out. 6. The act of twisting or turning. 7. Having sediment or foreign particles stirred up or suspended. 9. To impose oneself on others. 12. A turning or twisting force. 15. Difficult to understand. 16. A setting. 17. To twist, wrench, or bend severely out of shape. 18. To push or thrust out. 19. Having or marked by repeated turns or bends.

Down

1. An ostensible or professed purpose. 2. Stubborn; unruly. 4. A form of government in which the political authority exercises absolute and centralized control over all aspects of life. 8. To divert. 10. Unshakably calm and collected. 11. To misshape. 13. To jut out; to project. 14. To take away from; to reduce the value of.

Lesson XXII
ruptus, ultima, undare, urb-, uxor

RUPTUS
broken

ULTIMA
farthest; last; greatest

UNDARE
to wave or flow

URB-
city

UXOR
wife

abrupt, corrupt, disrupt, erupt, interrupt, rupture, penultimate, ultimate, ultimatum, abound, abundant, inundate, redound, redundant, undulate, undulating, suburban, urban, urbane, uxorious

Word Definitions

abrupt
adj. unexpectedly sudden; surprisingly curt
"His abrupt replies indicated his impatience with the conversation."
abruptly (adj.)
abruptus broken off: *ab-* away + *ruptus* broken (past participle of the verb *rumpere* to break; to destroy)

corrupt
adj. marked by immorality and perversion; depraved; dishonest; containing errors or alterations
v. to adulterate; to debase; to pervert
"Fertilizer run-off corrupted the town's water supply."
corruption (n.)
corruptus perverted; contaminated: *cor-* altogether + *ruptus* broken (past participle of the verb *rumpere* to break; to destroy)

disrupt
v. to throw into confusion or disorder; to impede the progress of
"The flow of traffic is disrupted when an accident occurs."
disruption (n.)
disruptus broken apart: *dis-* down from + *ruptus* broken (past participle of the verb *rumpere* to break; to destroy)

erupt
v. to emerge violently from restraint or limits; to explode
"The Old Faithful geyser at Yellowstone erupts on a regular schedule."
eruption (n.)

eruptus broken out: *ex-* out + *ruptus* broken (past participle of the verb *rumpere* to break; to destroy)

interrupt   v. to break the continuity or uniformity of; to hinder or break into an action, speech, or conversation
"The calm of the summer day was <u>interrupted</u> by a clap of thunder."
interruption (n.)
interruptus broken up: *inter-* between + *ruptus* broken (past participle of the verb *rumpere* to break; to destroy)

rupture   n. the process or instance of breaking open or bursting; a break in friendly relations
v. to break open; to burst
"A <u>ruptured</u> sewer main can have grave health consequences if it contaminates drinking water."
ruptus broken (past participle of the verb *rumpere* to break; to destroy)

penultimate   adj. next to last
"He'd hoped to have the last word, but had to settle for the <u>penultimate</u> word."
paenultima, -us next to last: *paene* almost + *ultimus, ultima* last

ultimate   adj. being or happening at the end of a process; being the best or most extreme example of its kind
"The Medal of Honor is the <u>ultimate</u> decoration awarded by the U.S. military."
ultima, -us last; farthest; greatest

ultimatum   n. a final statement of terms made by one party to another
"Attila's <u>ultimatum</u> to the Roman town defenders was to surrender or be slaughtered."
ultima, -us last; farthest; greatest

abound   v. to be great in number or amount; to be fully supplied or filled
"Because of over-fishing, cod no longer <u>abound</u> off the New England coast."
abundare to overflow: *ab-* away + *undare* to flow or surge

abundant   adj. plentiful; rich
"A bumper crop is an unusually <u>abundant</u> harvest."
abundance (n.)
abundatus overflowing: *ab-* away + *undatus* flowed (past participle of the verb *undare* to flow or surge)

inundate   v. to cover with water (especially floodwaters); to overwhelm
"During the Christmas season, the postal service is <u>inundated</u> with packages."
inundatus flooded: *in-* in + *undatus* surged (past participle of the verb *undare* to flow or surge)

redound	**v.** to have an effect or consequence; to return; to recoil upon "Glory redounds to the brave." *redundare* to overflow: *re-* back, again + *undare* to flow or surge
redundant	**adj.** exceeding what is necessary or natural; superfluous; needlessly repetitive or verbose "Specialized driver's education cars have redundant controls for the student and instructor." *redundancy (n.)* *redundare* to overflow: *re-* back, again + *undare* to flow or surge
undulate	**v.** to move in a smooth wavelike motion; to have a wavelike appearance or form; to increase or decrease in volume or pitch as if in waves "Her voice undulated soothingly with the music." *undulation (n.)* *undare* to flow or surge; to billow < *unda* wave
undulating	**adj.** having a wavy form, motion, or outline "The belly dancer's undulating hips, arms, and torso made for a seductive performance." *undare* to flow or surge; to billow < *unda* wave
suburban	**adj.** located or residing in a suburb (residential area or community outlying a city); characteristic of the suburbs "Suburban warriors held a paintball war in the town woods." *suburbium* suburb: *sub-* under, below + *urbs, urbis* city
urban	**adj.** of or located in a city; characteristic of the city or city life "Urban dwellers forgo the fresh air and broad lawns of the suburbs in exchange for greater convenience and cultural variety." *urbs, urbis* city
urbane	**adj.** polite, refined, and often elegant in manner "The Ivy League ideal is a gentleman of culture, etiquette, wit, and an urbane manner." *urbanus* of the city; courteous
uxorious	**adj.** excessively submissive or devoted to one's wife "Meek and uxorious Walter Mitty daydreams of heroism to escape from his wife's hen-pecking." *uxor* wife

Exercise A

Fill in the blanks in the sentences below with the correct form of a word in the scroll above.

1. On the Fourth of July each year, the skies _____ with fireworks.

2. The wave pool could produce everything from a gentle _____ pattern to fierce, huge waves.

3. Their passionate disagreements over the presidential candidates caused a temporary _____ in their friendship.

4. The _____ accolade of his illustrious career was winning the Nobel Prize for Literature.

5. An exhibit at the Museum of Science has a device that causes the water to _____, mimicking the action of ocean waves.

6. The students timed the demonstration to _____ the exam schedule.

7. His _____ generosity benefited many an impoverished family.

8. The _____ comma is the one before the "and" in a series, such as: Corn, barley, and wheat grew in abundance.

9. The widower, plagued with regrets that he had not sufficiently cherished his first wife, became downright _____ when he remarried.

10. The speaker said he would be happy to entertain questions at the end of the presentation, but requested that the audience not _____ him during the slide show.

11. Her _____ manner contrasted with the rustic crudeness of her suitor.

12. The dirt logging road wound through the woods for miles, then came to an _____ end at an illegal clear cut.

13. The generous community _____ the thrift shop with warm clothing.

14. The volcano was predicted to _____ about once every 500 years.

15. The political machine in Cook County, Illinois, was so _____ that holding a fair election was impossible.

16. Phrases like "abroad in foreign countries" and "In my opinion, I think" are inherently _____ , because similar ideas are repeated in close proximity.

17. Many couples who love the city when they're young end up migrating to _____ areas after they have children.

18. When you give your child an _____ about the consequences for unwanted behavior, it is important to follow through.

19. As cities become more crowded, _____ parks offer an increasingly important sense of space and respite for residents.

20. Deeds that _____ to one's credit will not soon be forgotten.

Exercise B

Match the word with the letter of its definition.

1. ___ abound
2. ___ abrupt
3. ___ abundant
4. ___ corrupt
5. ___ disrupt
6. ___ erupt
7. ___ interrupt
8. ___ inundate
9. ___ penultimate
10. ___ redound
11. ___ redundant
12. ___ rupture
13. ___ suburban
14. ___ ultimate
15. ___ ultimatum
16. ___ undulate
17. ___ undulating
18. ___ urban
19. ___ urbane
20. ___ uxorious

a) present in large quantities; plentiful
b) to break the continuous progress of
c) no longer needed or useful; superfluous
d) to return or recoil upon
e) showing excessive fondness for one's wife
f) to exist in large numbers or amounts
g) located in a residential area outlying a city
h) to burst out violently
i) sudden and unexpected; rude and curt
j) located in a city
k) to move with a smooth wavelike motion
l) marked by immorality and perversion
m) to throw into confusion or disorder
n) having a wavy form, motion, or outline
o) a final demand or statement of terms
p) to overwhelm as if with a flood
q) being or happening at the end of a process
r) to break or burst suddenly
s) next to last
t) polite, refined, and often elegant in manner

Exercise C

Solve the crossword puzzle.

Across

7. Exceeding what is necessary or natural; superfluous; needlessly repetitive or verbose.
8. Polite, refined, and often elegant in manner.
9. A final statement of terms made by one party to another.
11. Excessively submissive or devoted to one's wife.
13. The process or instance of breaking open or bursting; a break in friendly relations.
14. To cover with water (especially floodwaters); to overwhelm as if with a flood.
15. Of or located in a city; characteristic of the city or city life.
17. Plentiful; rich.
19. To have an effect or consequence; to return; to recoil upon.
20. Being or happening at the end of a process; highest or greatest.

Down

1. To be great in number or amount; to be fully supplied or filled.
2. Unexpectedly sudden; surprisingly curt.
3. To emerge violently from restraint or limits; to explode.
4. To break the continuity or uniformity of; to hinder or break into an action, speech, or conversation.
5. To move in a smooth wavelike motion; to have a wavelike appearance or form; to increase or decrease in volume or pitch as if in waves.
6. Next to last.
10. Marked by immorality and perversion; depraved; dishonest; containing errors or alterations.
12. Having a wavy form, motion, or outline.
16. Located or residing in a suburb (residential area or community outlying a city).
18. To throw into confusion or disorder.

Lesson XXIII

vac-/van-, vad-/vas-, valere, vendicare

VAC-, VAN-	**VAD-, VAS-**	**VALERE**	**VENDICARE**
empty	to go	to be strong	to avenge

evacuate, vacant, vacuous, vain, vanity, vaunt, evade, evasive, invade, invasion, pervade, pervasive, avail, convalesce, prevail, prevalent, valor, vendetta, vindicate, vindictive

Word Definitions

evacuate **v.** to remove from a place or area; to leave a place; to excrete waste matter from the body
"Expecting floods, the firefighters <u>evacuated</u> homes near the river."
evacuation (n.)
evacuare to empty out: *ex-* out of + *vacuare* to empty

vacant **adj.** empty; unfilled or unoccupied; lacking activity or emotion
"The movers left behind a house <u>vacant</u> of furnishings."
vacare to be empty, idle, or unoccupied

vacuous **adj.** devoid of matter, substance, or meaning; empty; stupid; lacking expression
"The claim that a viral cold results from wet hair on a cold day is <u>vacuous</u>."
vacuus, vacua empty; free of

vain **adj.** not yielding the desired outcome; fruitless; futile; excessively proud and conceited
"She was very <u>vain</u> of her appearance, but would have done better to cultivate her mind."
vanus, vana empty; vain; false

vanity **n.** the quality or condition of being vain; conceit; lack of usefulness, worth, or effect; a bathroom cabinet or dressing table, usually with a mirror
"<u>Vanity</u> was his downfall: He wrongly assumed everyone was as enamored of him as he was of himself."
vanus, vana empty; vain; false

vaunt	to speak boastfully of; brag about; a boastful remark; a speech of extravagant self-praise "Inscriptions on the colossal statues of Ramses <u>vaunt</u> the pharaoh's victories." *vanitare* to boast < *vanare* to utter empty words < *vanus, vana* empty
evade	**v.** to escape or avoid by cleverness or deceit; to avoid fulfilling, answering or performing; to elude "The purpose of camouflage is to <u>evade</u> detection by blending with the surroundings." *evasion (n.)* *evadere* to escape; to avoid: *e-, ex-* out of + *vadere* to go
evasive	**adj.** inclined or intended to evade; intentionally vague or ambiguous "To avoid the oncoming truck, he swerved his car in an <u>evasive</u> maneuver." *evadere* to escape; to avoid: *e-, ex-* out of + *vadere* to go
invade	**v.** to enter by force in order to conquer or pillage; to encroach or intrude on; to violate; to overrun or infest; to enter and permeate "Bacteria may <u>invade</u> a tooth's enamel to cause cavities." *invasion (n.)* *invadere* to enter; to attack: *in-* in + *vadere* to go; to hurry
invasion	**n.** to enter (usually by force) and take over a country, region, or body; an intrusion or encroachment "An <u>invasion</u> of crop-devouring locusts, coupled with drought, has led to widespread famine in Niger." *invadere* to enter; to attack: *in-* in + *vadere* to go; to hurry
pervade	**v.** to be present throughout; to permeate or penetrate "Rot <u>pervaded</u> the ancient timbers, which were also infested with termites." *pervadere* to spread through: *per-* through + *vadere* to go
pervasive	**adj.** having the quality or tendency to pervade or permeate "The <u>pervasive</u> odor of garlic emanated from the kitchen." *pervadere* to spread through: *per-* through + *vadere* to go
avail	**v.** to be of use or advantage; to help; to benefit from "The Roman infantryman <u>availed</u> himself of a short-sword and protective buckler." *valere* to be strong; to be of value; to be healthy
convalesce	**v.** to return to health and strength after an illness; to recuperate "A sanatorium is a facility for <u>convalescing</u> tuberculosis patients." *convalescere* to gain strength or power; to recover (from illness): *con-* altogether + *valescere* to grow in health or strength
prevail	**v.** to be greater in strength or influence; to triumph or win; to predominate "After whining and pleading, he <u>prevailed</u> on his mother to buy the toy." *praevalere* to have superior power: *prae-* before + *valere* to be strong

prevalent	**adj.** widely or commonly occurring, existing, accepted, or practiced "Islam is the <u>prevalent</u> religion of the Arab countries and Indonesia." *praevalere* to have superior power: *prae-* before + *valere* to be strong
valor	**n.** courage and boldness; bravery "The Medal of <u>Valor</u> is awarded for conspicuous bravery in action." *valere* to be strong
vendetta	**n.** a feud between two families or clans, often bitter and destructive; a personal feud characterized by plans or acts of revenge "Mafia families are notorious for their deadly rivalries and <u>vendettas</u>." *vindicata* vengeance; a claim
vindicate	**v.** to clear of accusation, blame, suspicion or doubt with supporting evidence or proof; to justify or support; to defend, maintain, or lay claim to recognition of one's rights; to exact revenge for (something), thereby restoring justice "Galileo's astronomical observations <u>vindicated</u> Copernicus's controversial theory that the Earth revolves around the sun." *vindication (n.)* *vindicatus* vindicated (past participle of the verb *vindicare* to claim; to vindicate; to avenge)
vindictive	**adj.** disposed to seek revenge; spiteful "The desire to get even is a <u>vindictive</u> response." *vindicare* to claim; to vindicate; to avenge

Exercise A

Fill in the blanks in the sentences below with the correct form of a word in the scroll above.

1. The police officer received an award from the governor for his _____ in rescuing the family from their burning home.

2. The one thing that I cannot tolerate is an _____ of my privacy.

3. The disease-carrying mosquitoes were so _____ that chemical spraying was the only realistic and practical way to eradicate them.

4. The teacher asked about her homework assignment, but the tardy student tried to _____ the question by inquiring about the test.

5. If you don't act deferential toward the boss's secretary, she can become very _____ and make it difficult for you to speak with him.

6. We were surprised to see the contractor's equipment arrive, because the overgrown lot had been _____ for so long.

7. Clostridium dificile bacteria are so _____ that every hospital room has to be wiped down with bleach between patients, and even so, some are infected.

8. When the United States _____ Iraq, the army and people offered little resistance – but the occupation was another matter.

9. The original suspect's claims of innocence were _____ when another man confessed to the crime.

10. When the officer told Mrs. Bazzi that her only son had been killed by a roadside bomb in Baghdad, the shock appeared to drain her face of all life, leaving her with a _____ expression and deadened eyes.

11. Nothing _____ in his efforts to revive the dying woman.

12. The new administrator never neglected to _____ his accomplishments in previous positions.

13. Before the hurricane was expected to make landfall, the residents were required to _____ their homes and move inland.

14. The Montagues and Capulets had a mutual _____ that had lasted for ages, yet they remembered the start of the feud as if it happened yesterday.

15. Four of her seven children are _____ from the measles, and the other three have just come down with it.

16. The Coast Guard tried in _____ to save the boat from washing ashore and breaking apart on the rocks.

17. Long after the fire was extinguished, the odor of charred timber and smoke _____ the ruin.

18. Louise, although usually very straightforward, was _____ about her exact plans for the day because she was planning a surprise party for him.

19. The odds were not in their favor, but the soccer team still hoped to _____ against their more highly ranked rivals.

20. Greg's _____ about his prowess with the ladies suffered only a temporary setback when his girlfriend turned down his marriage proposal.

Exercise B

Match the word with the letter of its definition.

1. ___ avail
2. ___ convalesce
3. ___ evacuate
4. ___ evade
5. ___ evasive
6. ___ invade
7. ___ invasion
8. ___ pervade
9. ___ pervasive
10. ___ prevail
11. ___ prevalent
12. ___ vacant
13. ___ vacuous
14. ___ vain
15. ___ valor
16. ___ vanity
17. ___ vaunt
18. ___ vendetta
19. ___ vindicate
20. ___ vindictive

a) a feud between two families or clans
b) to be greater in strength or influence; to triumph
c) permeating; existing or spreading throughout
d) to spread or be present throughout
e) fruitless or futile; conceited
f) devoid of matter, meaning, or expression
g) to remove from a place or area (for safety)
h) having or showing a strong desire for revenge
i) to encroach or intrude on
j) the quality or condition of being vain
k) to recuperate from an illness
l) widely occurring, existing, or accepted
m) to boast of or brag about
n) courage and boldness
o) intentionally vague or ambiguous
p) to be of use or advantage; to help; to use to advantage
q) an unwelcome intrusion or encroachment
r) to escape or avoid by cleverness or deceit
s) containing nothing; unfilled or unoccupied
t) to clear of blame and suspicion

Exercise C

Solve the crossword puzzle.

Across
2. To enter by force in order to conquer or pillage; to encroach or intrude on; to violate; to overrun or infest; to enter and permeate. 3. Excessive pride in one's appearance or accomplishments; conceit; lack of usefulness, worth, or effect; a bathroom cabinet, usually with a mirror. 5. Inclined or intended to evade; intentionally vague or ambiguous. 9. Devoid of matter, substance or meaning; devoid of expression; idle; stupid. 10. Courage and boldness. 11. Disposed to seek revenge; spiteful. 15. To remove from a place or area (to a safer place); to leave a place; to excrete waste matter from the body. 16. To be present or spread throughout. 17. To be greater in strength or influence; to triumph or win; to predominate. 18. To clear of accusation, blame, suspicion or doubt with supporting evidence or proof; to provide justification or support for; to defend, claim, or insist on recognition of one's rights; to exact revenge for (something), restoring justice.

Down
1. To return to health and strength after an illness. 2. An instance of invading a country or region; an intrusion or encroachment. 4. Having the quality or tendency to pervade or permeate. 6. Widely or commonly occurring, existing, accepted, or practiced. 7. Not yielding the desired outcome; lacking substance or worth; futile; conceited; without success. 8. To be of use or advantage; to use to one's advantage. 10. Containing nothing; unfilled or unoccupied. 12. To escape or avoid by cleverness or deceit; to avoid fulfilling, answering or performing; to elude. 13. To speak boastfully of or brag about; a boastful remark; a speech of extravagant self-praise. 14. A feud between two families or clans.

Lesson XXIV
veni-/vent-, ventus, ver-/vera-/veri-, vorare

VENI-/VENT-	VENTUS	VER-, VERA-,	VORARE
to come	wind	VERI-	to devour
		true	

advent, circumvent, contravene, convene, convenience, convention, event, intervene, prevent, preventive, venue, vent, ventilate, aver, veracious, veracity, verify, verisimilitude, veritable, verity

Word Definitions

advent **n.** a coming or arrival; the liturgical period preceding Christmas
"The advent of a reliable chronometer allowed ships to determine their longitude, greatly improving navigation."
adventus arrival; approach < *advenire* to come to: *ad-* to + *venire* to come

circumvent **v.** to go around or bypass; to avoid or to get around by artful maneuvering; to surround and entrap (as in a military maneuver)
"He circumvented the normal job requirements, thanks to his uncle, who is the firm's chief financial officer."
circumvenire to encircle; to assail; to trick: *circum-* around + *venire* to come

contravene **v.** to act or be counter to; to violate; to oppose in argument
"The soldier was court-martialed for contravening a direct order."
contravenire to transgress; to oppose: *contra-* against + *venire* to come

convene **v.** to come together, usually for an official or public purpose; to assemble; to cause or summon to appear
"The family convenes for a turkey dinner at Thanksgiving."
convenire to assemble: *con-* together + *venire* to come

convenience **n.** freedom from effort or difficulty
"For an Eskimo, a refrigerator is a superfluous convenience."
convenire to assemble: *con-* together + *venire* to come

convention	n. a formal meeting of members, representatives, or delegates; the body of persons attending such an assembly; a broadly accepted or used custom, technique, or protocol "Cadets at military academies are expected to follow strict <u>conventions</u> of dress and behavior." *conventum* agreement; covenant; convention < *convenire* to assemble
event	n. an occurrence; a social gathering or activity; the final result or outcome; a contest or item in a sports competition "Figure skating is one of the most popular <u>events</u> in the Winter Olympics." *evenire* to happen; to come out: *e-, ex-* out + *venire* to come.
intervene	v. to come between so as to prevent or alter something "A social worker may <u>intervene</u> when child abuse is suspected." *intervenire* to come between; to come up: *inter-* between + *venire* to come
prevent	v. to keep from happening or arising; to keep someone from doing something; to impede or present an obstacle "He tried to <u>prevent</u> her from attempting the black diamond trail, but she was determined to test her skiing prowess." *prevention (n.)* *praevenire* to forestall or hinder; to precede: *prae-* before + *venire* to come
preventive	adj. intended or used to prevent or hinder; carried out to deter something or someone bad from attacking or gaining ground "Consumption of a daily baby aspirin is a <u>preventive</u> measure against heart attacks." *praevenire* to forestall or hinder; to precede: *prae-* before + *venire* to come
venue	n. the locality where a crime is committed or a cause of action occurs "The trial was moved to another <u>venue</u> because news coverage of the crime where it had occurred had biased the potential jury pool there." *venire* to come
vent	v. to release or discharge through an opening; to express or release pent-up emotions n. a means of escape or release from confinement, an outlet; an opening permitting the escape of fumes, a liquid, a gas, or steam "The sea god Poseidon <u>vented</u> his fury at his son's blinding by shipwrecking Odysseus." *ventus* wind
ventilate	v. to admit fresh air into; to circulate through and freshen; to expose to public discussion or examination "It's especially important to <u>ventilate</u> modern office buildings properly, as many have energy-efficient windows that cannot be opened." *ventilare* to expose to a draft; to fan < *ventus* wind
aver	v. to affirm positively; to declare or assert as a fact; to justify "The parliamentarian <u>averred</u> that the speaker hadn't been recognized and

	was therefore out of order." *ad-* to + *verus, vera* true; genuine; right; fair
veracious	**adj.** honest and truthful; accurate "The witness was <u>veracious</u>, although the defense attorney did his best to throw doubt on her credibility." *verus, vera* true; genuine; right; fair
veracity	**adj.** adherence to the truth or fact; accuracy or precision "Most Venetians doubted the <u>veracity</u> of Marco Polo's account of his travels to the east." *verus, vera* true; genuine; right; fair
verify	**v.** to prove the truth of with evidence or testimony; to substantiate; to determine or test the truth or accuracy of by comparison or investigation "Many scientific theories aren't <u>verified</u> by observation and experimentation until years after their formulation." *verification (n.)* *veri-* true + *facere* to make; to do
verisimilitude	**n.** the quality of appearing to be true or real "Andrew Wyeth's paintings combine <u>verisimilitude</u> of form with subtle moods conveyed through his choice of palette." *veri-* true + *similis* similar
veritable	**adj.** truly so called; real, genuine, or actual "Pablo Casals is a <u>veritable</u> master of the cello and guitar." *verus* true; genuine
verity	**n.** the quality or state of being true, factual, or real; a true principal or belief "Ancient verities such as the 'Golden Rule' form the cornerstone of most major religions." *veritas* truth; fact; accuracy < *verus* true
voracious	**adj.** wanting or devouring great quantities (of something); very hungry "A bookworm is a reader with a voracious <u>appetite</u> for good books." *voracity (n.)* *vorare* to devour; to swallow

Exercise A

Fill in the blanks in the sentences below with the correct form of a word in the scroll above.

1. The most popular _____ of the season was a grand ball on New Year's Eve.

2. To make matters more confusing, the detective was able to _____ the alibis of all the suspects.

3. Anna Anderson _____ that she was Anastasia, the youngest daughter of Czar Nicholas II, but investigators believe she was actually a factory worker.

4. The museum president had to _____ because the architect and the builder were not seeing eye-to-eye on how to carry out the renovations.

5. We _____ the city on a bypass, so as to avoid heavy traffic.

6. The _____ of that portrait is amazing; it's true to life!

7. The 1968 Democratic _____ in Chicago was marked by protests, riots, and a brutal police response.

8. He sometimes sacrifices _____ in his efforts to appear in the best light.

9. The _____ for the 1994 World Cup was Foxboro Stadium.

10. With the _____ of the cotton gin, the production of linen in the United States decreased dramatically.

11. When the windows were opened, the cool evening breezes helped to _____ and refresh the house.

12. In her memoir, she gave a _____ account of her addiction treatment, although she changed the names of some people to protect their privacy.

13. The constitutional convention will _____ the day after tomorrow.

14. "Those who live by the sword, die by the sword" is a well-known _____ .

15. She tried to _____ bad weather from spoiling the wedding reception by putting a large tent over the food, the tables, and part of the lawn.

16. The party invitation concluded with: "The favor of a reply is requested at your earliest _____."

17. To _____ the treaties meant bloodshed and a risk of losing further territory.

18. People often _____ their frustrations after a disappointing or difficult experience.

19. _____ medical care can help people avoid serious illness – or at least catch many conditions before they become life-threatening.

20. There was a _____ explosion in oil prices, leading energy stocks to post record gains.

Exercise B

Match the word with the letter of its definition.

1. ___ advent
2. ___ aver
3. ___ circumvent
4. ___ contravene
5. ___ convene
6. ___ convenience
7. ___ convention
8. ___ event
9. ___ intervene
10. ___ prevent
11. ___ preventive
12. ___ vent
13. ___ ventilate
14. ___ venue
15. ___ veracious
16. ___ veracity
17. ___ verify
18. ___ verisimilitude
19. ___ veritable
20. ___ verity

a) an occurrence; an entertainment
b) to come between to prevent or alter something
c) a principal or belief
d) the location where something takes place
e) to keep (something bad) from happening or arising
f) freedom from effort or difficulty
g) to come or bring together for an activity
h) genuine; actual
i) to express pent-up thoughts or feelings
j) the quality of appearing to be true or real
k) to go around; to evade; to surround
l) designed to prevent (something) from occurring
m) to state or assert to be the case
n) a way in which something is usually done
o) to offend against the requirements of; to violate
p) honest, truthful
q) to cause air to enter and flow freely
r) adherence to the truth
s) to make sure that something is true
t) an approach or arrival

Exercise C

Solve the crossword puzzle.

Across
1. To come between; to enter into (something) in order to resolve it or prevent an undesirable outcome. 3. To assemble, usually for an official or public purpose; to cause to convene; to summon to appear. 5. To surround, enclose or entrap; to bypass; to avoid or get around by artful maneuvering. 9. To express pent-up thoughts or feelings; a conduit for air, heat, etc. 10. Intended or used to prevent or hinder (attack, disease, etc.). 12. Honest, truthful; accurate, precise. 13. To affirm positively; to declare or assert as fact; to justify. 14. Freedom from effort or difficulty. 15. To keep from happening or arising; to keep someone from doing something; to impede or present an obstacle. 17. To act or be counter to; to violate; to oppose in argument. 18. The quality of appearing to be true or real.

Down
2. To admit fresh air into; to circulate through and freshen; to expose to public discussion or examination. 4. Being truly so called; real, genuine, or actual. 6. A coming or arrival; the liturgical period preceding Christmas. 7. A formal meeting of members, representatives, or delegates; the body of persons attending such an assembly; general agreement on or acceptance of certain practices or attitudes; a widely accepted custom or technique. 8. To prove the truth of with evidence or testimony; to substantiate; to determine or test the truth of by comparison or investigation. 9. The location where a crime is committed, or an action or performance occurs. 11. The quality or state of being true, factual, or real; a true principal or belief. 12. Adherence to the truth; conformity to fact; accuracy and precision. 16. An occurrence; a social gathering or activity.

Lesson XXV
verbum, vert-/vers-, via

VERBUM
word

VERT-, VERS-
to turn

VIA
way, road, journey

verbal, verbatim, verbose, adverse, aversion, adversity, avert, controversy, convert, divert, diversion, introvert, pervert, revert, versatile, vertigo, deviate, deviation, devious, viaduct

Word Definitions

verbal
adj. of, relating to, or associated with words; consisting of only words without action; spoken rather than written
"Gestures, body language, and facial expressions are non-<u>verbal</u> forms of communication."
verbum word

verbatim
adj. using exactly the same words; corresponding word for word
"A transcript is a written, <u>verbatim</u> account of an oral presentation."
verbum word

verbose
adj. containing a great and usually excessive number of words; wordy
"'<u>Verbose</u>,' 'prolix,' and 'windy' are all synonyms that can describe someone who talks too much about too little."
verbum word

adverse
adj. acting or serving to oppose; antagonistic; contrary to one's interests or welfare; harmful or unfavorable
"A series of <u>adverse</u> events – his job loss and her mounting medical bills – resulted in homelessness for their family."
advertere to turn toward; to face or confront: *ad-* toward + *vertere* to turn

adversity
n. a state of hardship or affliction
"Hannibal's elephants faced the <u>adversities</u> of snow and steep terrain to cross the Alps."
advertere to turn toward; to face or confront: *ad-* toward- + *vertere* to turn

aversion
n. a fixed, intense dislike; repugnance; avoidance of something because of its association with an unpleasant or painful stimulus
"Holding one's nose is a common gesture showing <u>aversion</u> to a smell."
averse (adj.)
avertere to turn away from; to withdraw: *a-* from + *vertere* to turn

avert	**v.** to turn away; to ward off; to avoid "When getting a shot, most patients <u>avert</u> their eyes." *avertere* to turn away from; to withdraw: *a-* from + *vertere* to turn
controversy	**n.** prolonged public disagreement or heated debate "The selectmen tabled the proposal to give both sides in the <u>controversy</u> time to cool off." *controversial (adj.)* *vertere* to turn
convert	**v.** to change or to cause to change in form, character, or function; to change one's religious beliefs "Paul <u>converted</u> Jews and gentiles alike to a belief in Christ's divinity." *conversion (n.)* *convertere* to turn about or backward; to transpose or translate: *con-* with + *vertere* to turn
divert	**v.** to turn aside from a course of action or direction; to distract "To water his crops, he <u>diverts</u> river water into irrigation canals." *diversion (n.)* *divertere* to turn aside: *dis-* down from; aside + *vertere* to turn
diversion	**n.** the act or instance of diverting or turning aside; something that distracts the mind and relaxes or entertains; "After a demanding day of work, many people find <u>diversion</u> in television." *divertere* to turn aside: *dis-* down from; aside + *vertere* to turn
introvert	**v.** to turn or direct inward; to focus on oneself **n.** a shy person "'<u>Introvert</u>' was Carl Jung's term for a personality focused or concentrated inward, or people who preferred solitude to socializing." *introversion (n.)* *introvertere* to turn within: *intro-* to the inside + *vertere* to turn
pervert	**v.** to cause to turn away from what is right, proper, or good; to corrupt; to debase; to misuse **n.** someone with socially unacceptable or harmful sexual impulses "He twisted and <u>perverted</u> logic to justify his abhorrent behavior." *perversion (n.)* *pervertere* to corrupt; to overthrow: *per-* through or thoroughly + *vertere* to turn
revert	**v.** to return to a previous state or condition "Through hypnosis, a patient may <u>revert</u> to childhood." *reversion (n.)* *revertere* to turn back; to return: *re-* back, again + *vertere* to turn
vertigo	**n.** a sensation of dizziness "Some people experience <u>vertigo</u> because of inner ear problems that affect their sense of balance." *vertere* to turn

versatile	**adj.** capable of doing many things competently "A decathelete must be <u>versatile</u> to compete in ten different track and field events." *versare* to revolve; to spin; to maneuver
deviate	**v.** to turn or cause to turn aside from a course or way; to depart from a norm; to stray "A car that repeatedly <u>deviates</u> from its lane may have a drunken driver." *deviation (n.)* *deviare* to detour or stray; to depart from: *de-* down, from + *via* way; road
deviation	**n.** the act of deviating or turning aside, an abnormality, a departure "A detour is a temporary <u>deviation</u> from the normal route." *deviare* to detour or stray; to depart from: *de-* down, from + *via* way; road
devious	**adj.** not straightforward; shifty; departing from the correct or accepted way "The <u>devious</u> wolf donned grandmother's clothes to hoodwink Red Riding Hood." *devius, devia* remote; devious; shy: *de-* down, from + *via* way; road
viaduct	**n.** a series of spans or arches used to carry a road or railroad over a wide valley or over other roads or railroads "The new Copenhagen-Malmö span is a multi-mile, two-tiered bridge and <u>viaduct</u>." *via* way; road + *ductare* to lead

Exercise A

Fill in the blanks in the sentences below with the correct form of a word in the scroll above.

1. In the fall, we _____ from Daylight Savings Time to standard time.

2. Quoting a comment out of context can _____ its true meaning.

3. The local roads were somewhat precarious, so it was imperative not to _____ from the planned highway route.

4. The construction crew was pleased to learn that the new _____ would take at least a year to complete.

5. He had an _____ to the smell of chlorine after his summer as a lifeguard, when it seemed he could never get the chemical odor out of his skin and hair.

6. The sailors first tried to _____ their faces from the stinging spray, before finally deciding to go below decks.

7. He likes to _____ his friends by performing impressions of his favorite actors.

8. Betsey was a _____ cook, making a gourmet French meal one night, then a hearty peasant stew or a vegetarian curry the next.

9. A handshake and our _____ agreement to share the costs equally were all that we needed to confirm the arrangements.

10. The used car salesperson used _____ tactics to pass off a "lemon" as a reliable car.

11. The architect suggested to the homeowners that they _____ their attic into a guest room.

12. He hoped the _____ from his usual after-work routine would help him elude any pursuers.

13. It was tedious to listen to the lengthy and _____ time-share sales pitch, but we stayed for the promised free television.

14. The travel agent, who occasionally suffered from _____ in high places, nonetheless took a tour of several lighthouses.

15. Hope overcame _____ to gain admission to Yale University, based on her incredible stamina, hard work, and sterling character.

16. In the world of entertainment marketing, there's almost no such thing as a bad _____, since such disputes result in free publicity.

17. When the editor read the article, he realized that the author had plagiarized it _____.

18. The bank robbers planted someone to create a _____ so they could escape with the money before anyone realized what they were really doing.

19. Some felt that if the accountant were not such an _____, his social life might be more active.

20. The teacher's _____ comments on the student's essay forever deterred her from pursuing a career as a writer.

169

Exercise B

Match the word with the letter of its definition.

1. ___ adverse
2. ___ aversion
3. ___ adversity
4. ___ avert
5. ___ controversy
6. ___ convert
7. ___ deviate
8. ___ deviation
9. ___ devious
10. ___ divert
11. ___ diversion
12. ___ introvert
13. ___ pervert
14. ___ revert
15. ___ verbal
16. ___ verbatim
17. ___ verbose
18. ___ versatile
19. ___ vertigo
20. ___ viaduct

a) a shy, reticent person
b) not straightforward; shifty
c) a fixed, intense dislike
d) to change in form, character, or function
e) a sensation of dizziness
f) corresponding word for word
g) to distract
h) acting or serving to oppose
i) something that distracts
j) to diverge from an established course
k) a state of hardship or affliction
l) to return to a previous state or condition
m) an abnormality; a departure from the accepted way
n) to turn away; to avoid
o) prolonged public disagreement or debate
p) a long bridge-like structure carrying a road or railroad
q) using an excessive number of words
r) capable of doing many things competently
s) consisting only of words
t) to corrupt or debase

Exercise C

Solve the crossword puzzle.

Across
1. Using exactly the same words; corresponding word for word. 7. The act of deviating or turning aside; a departure from the normal. 10. To turn or cause to turn aside from a course or way; to depart from a norm, stray. 12. To cause to turn away from what is right, proper, or good; to corrupt or debase. 13. Containing a great (usually excessive) number of words; wordy. 14. The act or instance of diverting or turning aside; something that distracts the mind and relaxes or entertains. 15. To turn or direct inward; to focus on oneself. 17. Capable of doing many things competently. 18. A series of spans or arches used to carry a road or railroad over a wide valley or over other roads or railroads.

Down
2. Acting or serving to oppose; contrary to one's interests or welfare; harmful or unfavorable. 3. To return to a previous state or condition. 4. A state of hardship or affliction. 5. Prolonged public disagreement or heated debate. 6. Not straightforward; shifty; departing from the correct or accepted way. 8. To turn away; to ward off. 9. A fixed, intense dislike; repugnance; avoidance of something because of its association with an unpleasant or painful stimulus. 11. To change or cause to change in form, character, or function; to change one's religious beliefs. 13. A sensation of dizziness. 14. To turn aside from a course of action or direction; to distract. 16. Of, relating to, or associated with words; consisting only of words not action; spoken rather than written.

Lesson XXVI
vid-/vis-, vigilare, vinc-/vict/-vanq-

VID-, VIS-	**VIGILARE**	**VINC-, VICT-, VANQ-**
to see	to watch	to conquer

evidence, evident, improvise, invisible, envision, providence, revise, supervise, visage, visibility, visionary, visual, visualize, surveillance, vigil, vigilant, evict, invincible, vanquish, victory

Word Definitions

evidence
n. a fact, situation, or object that is helpful in forming a conclusion or judgment; witness testimony; an outward sign
"The dark bags under her eyes were evidence of insomnia."
evidens, evidentis obvious to the eye or mind: *ex-* out + *videre* to see

evident
adj. easily seen or understood; plain or obvious; clear
"Something patently obvious and requiring no explanation is self-evident."
evidens, evidentis obvious to the eye or mind: *ex-* out + *videre* to see

improvise
v. to invent or perform with little or no preparation; to do something extemporaneously
"A prisoner improvised a rope from torn bed sheets to drop himself down the wall."
improvisation (n.)
improvisus unexpected; unforeseen: *im-* + *provisus* (past participle of *providere* to foresee)

invisible
adj. impossible to see; inaccessible to view; hidden
"The highway lines became invisible as the fog rolled in."
invisibility (n.)
invisibil, invisibilis invisible; spiritual: *in-* not + *visibilis* visible < *videre* to see

envision
v. to picture in the mind; to imagine
"In his meditation, he envisioned a world without war."
en- in + *visio, visionis* vision < *videre* to see

172

providence	**n.** care arising from forethought; prudence; divine care or guidance "A bountiful harvest and good health were signs to the Pilgrims of divine providence." *providere* to foresee; to provide for: *pro-* foreward + *videre* to see
revise	**v.** to reconsider and change (usually to improve) "An editor's task is to revise a manuscript for publication." *revision (n.)* *revisere* to revisit: *re-* again + *videre* to see
supervise	**v.** to observe and direct the execution or performance of; to oversee "Gen. Dwight D. Eisenhower planned and supervised the D-Day invasion." *supervision (n.)* *supervidere* to oversee: *super-* over + *videre* to see
visage	**n.** the face or facial expression of a person; countenance; appearance "Medusa's visage was so horrible that those who saw her were paralyzed." *visus* sight; appearance
visibility	**n.** the state of being visible; the distance one can see under particular conditions of light and weather "Politicians need to maximize their media visibility to get elected." *visibilis* visible < *videre* to see
visionary	**v.** characterized by vision or foresight; existing in the imagination only "The Internet, once a visionary dream, has transformed communication." *visio, visionis* vision < *videre* to see
visual	**adj.** of or relating to the sense of sight; seen or able to be seen by sight alone "Semaphores are colored flags used for visual signaling at sea." *visio, visionis* vision < *videre* to see
visualize	**v.** to form a mental image; to make visible "Daydreaming in his office cubicle, John visualized a romantic evening with Mabel." *visio, visionis* vision < *videre* to see
surveillance	**n.** observation of a person or group; oversight "Surveillance cameras are mounted in stores to discourage and detect shoplifters." *sur-* over + *vigilare* to keep awake; to watch < *vigil* watchman; sentry
vigil	**n.** a period of staying awake during the time usually spent asleep, especially to watch or pray over a dead body; a peaceful demonstration in support of a cause "She kept vigil through the night over her dying husband." *vigil* awake; watchful
vigilant	**adj.** keeping aware of possible danger or difficulties "A sentry's duty is to remain vigilant against the enemy."."

	vigilance (n.) *vigilare* to keep awake; to watch < *vigil* sentry; watchman
evict	**v.** to forcibly remove someone or something from a place "The Pied Piper was hired by the town of Hamelin to <u>evict</u> all the rats." *eviction (n.)* *evincere* to overcome; to prevail: *ex-* out + *vincere* to conquer
invincible	**adj.** incapable of being overcome or defeated; unconquerable "The supposedly <u>invincible</u> Maginot Line proved easy to circumvent." *invincibility (n.)* *in-* not + *vincere* to conquer
vanquish	**v.** to defeat or conquer; to subjugate; to overcome or subdue "The chess grandmaster <u>vanquished</u> 20 opponents simultaneously in an exhibition match." *vincere* to conquer
victory	**n.** the defeat of an enemy or opponent; success in a struggle against difficulties or an obstacle. *victorious (adj.)* "A phyrric <u>victory</u> is one so costly that it is ruinous." *victoria* victory < *vincere* to overcome; to conquer

Exercise A

Fill in the blanks in the sentences below with the correct form of a word in the scroll above.

1. The scientist used a microscope to view bacteria that were _____ to the naked eye.

2. Since the terrorist attacks of Sept. 11, 2001, police and camera _____ has greatly increased at public places, especially for major events.

3. The _____ of the Mona Lisa is haunting and enigmatic.

4. If _____ had not sent a group of well-provisioned settlers their way, the pioneers surely would have starved to death before spring.

5. To _____ their enemies, the Romans had to be both cunning and skillful.

6. When visiting the Great Hall at Hampton Court Palace, I tried to _____ life in England during the reign of King Henry VIII.

7. When the ski patrol arrived, it was _____ that the injured skier had lost control on the ice slope and struck a tree.

8. A car design that optimizes _____ in all directions is an important factor to consider when buying a new car.

9. A prayer vigil _____ was held outside the girl's home the night after she was abducted.

10. Thomas Edison was not only an inventor, but a _____ who understood the significance of making electric service a part of municipal infrastructure.

11. Looking at the junk-filled vacant lot, it was difficult for the company's employees to _____ their new headquarters.

12. The landlord won a court order requiring police to _____ his tenants several months after they stopped paying their rent.

13. In spite of historic documentation, there was insufficient archaeological _____ to determine the exact location of the granary.

14. The chef was _____ about the cleanliness of his restaurant and freshness of all his ingredients.

15. _____ at sea was the primary means of conquering new territory in the colonial era.

16. During the storm, the vacationers lost electricity and were forced to _____ a dinner that could be cooked over a fire.

17. Would-be military pilots must have great _____ acuity.

18. Superman seems _____ in his role of hero, while his alter-ego, Clark Kent, appears weak and ineffective.

19. The professor asked some of the students to _____ their term papers for grammar and organization.

20. The counselors took turns instructing and _____ the campers.

Exercise B

Match the word with the letter of its definition.

1. ___ envision
2. ___ evict
3. ___ evidence
4. ___ evident
5. ___ improvise
6. ___ invincible
7. ___ invisible
8. ___ providence
9. ___ revise
10. ___ supervise
11. ___ surveillance
12. ___ vanquish
13. ___ victory
14. ___ vigil
15. ___ vigilant
16. ___ visage
17. ___ visibility
18. ___ visionary
19. ___ visual
20. ___ visualize

a) a watch kept at night
b) to observe and direct (something or someone)
c) triumph over an opponent
d) to create, perform, or act spontaneously
e) the fact, state, or degree of being visible
f) close observation (especially of someone suspicious)
g) to expel someone from a property or place
h) on the alert; watchful against possible danger
i) to form a mental image; to make visible
j) impossible to see
k) to imagine; to see in one's mind
l) relating to sight
m) easily seen or understood
n) to examine and change or improve
o) someone who can see clearly into the future
p) impossible to defeat
q) care or preparation in advance; divine forethought or guidance
r) to conquer
s) the face or facial expression of a person; appearance
t) information helpful in forming a conclusion or judgment

Exercise C

Solve the crossword puzzle.

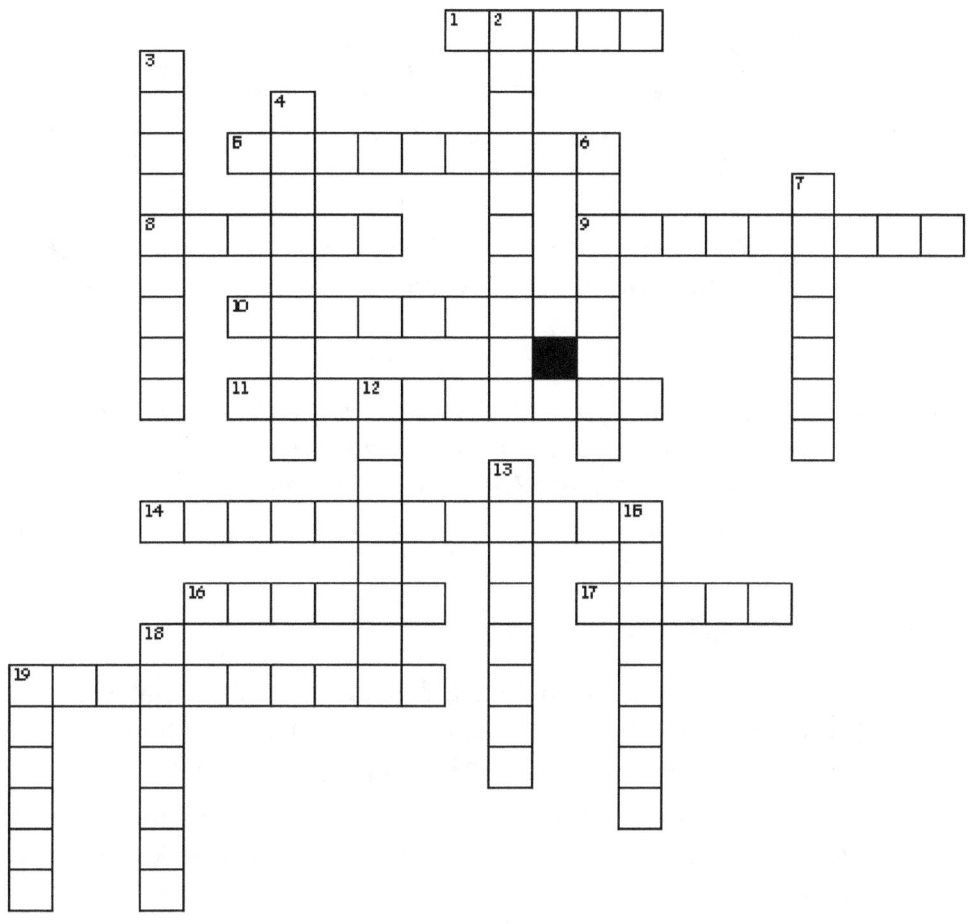

Across
1. A period of staying awake at night, especially to watch or pray; a peaceful demonstration in support of a cause. 5. To form a mental image; to make visible. 8. To reconsider and change or improve. 9. To invent, compose, or perform with little or no preparation. 10. Impossible to see; not accessible to view; hidden. 11. Care or preparation in advance; forethought. 14. Observation of a person or group under suspicion. 16. Of or relating to the sense of sight; able to be perceived by sight only. 17. To expel someone or something from a place. 19. The state of being visible; the distance one can see, based on light and weather conditions.

Down
2. Incapable of being overcome or defeated; unconquerable. 3. To observe and direct the execution of (something). 4. Characterized by vision or foresight; existing in the imagination only. 6. A thing or things that are helpful in forming a conclusion or judgment; an outward sign. 7. Easily seen or understood; plain or obvious. 12. Careful and watchful for possible danger or difficulties. 13. To defeat or conquer. 15. To picture in the mind. 18. Triumph defeat over an enemy or opponent; success in a struggle against difficulties or an obstacle. 19. Face; countenance; appearance.

Lesson XXVII
viv-/vita, voc-/vox, velle/vol-, volvere

VIV-/VITA
to live; life

VOC-/VOX
to call; voice

VELE, VOL-
wish

VOLVERE
to roll

convivial, survival, survive, vitality, vivacious, advocate, avocation, convoke, evoke, invoke, provoke, vocation, vociferous, volition, voluntary, convolution, devolve, evolve, revolve, voluble

Word Definitions

convivial adj. fond of feasting, drinking, and good company; sociable; merry
"Games, good food, and convivial company made the cookout enjoyable."
convivium banquet or feast; guests at a party: *con-* with- + *vivere* to live

survival n. the act or process of remaining alive; the fact of having endured
"'Robinson Crusoe' is probably based on Alexander Selkirk's survival as a castaway on a South Sea island for more than four years."
supervivere to survive; to outlive: *super-* beyond + *vivere* to live

survive v. to remain alive or in existence; to outlive; to persevere; to remain functional or stable
"A widower is a husband who survives his wife."
supervivere to survive; to outlive: *super-* beyond + *vivere* to live

vitality n. the capacity to live and grow; vigor or energy; the ability to survive
"Repeated bouts of Lyme disease drained her vitality."
vital (adj.)
vita life

vivacious adj. full of animation and spirit; lively
"Lucille Ball was the vivacious comedienne who starred in 'I Love Lucy.'"
vivacity (n.)
vivere to live

advocate n. a person who publicly supports or recommends a particular cause or policy; a person who pleads a case on someone else's behalf
v. to recommend publicly or support

"A defense lawyer serves as the accused criminal's <u>advocate</u>."
advocation (n.)
advocare to summon; to call as counsel: *ad-* toward + *vocare* to call

avocation   **n.** a hobby or minor occupation
"Benjamin Franklin was a printer for whom invention was a mere <u>avocation</u>."
avocare to call away; to distract: *a-* away + *vocare* to call

convoke   **v.** to call together (an assembly or meeting)
"The leader of the underground resistance <u>convoked</u> a council of war."
convocation (n.)
convocare to call together; to collect: *con-* together + *vocare* to call

evoke   **v.** to bring or recall to the conscious mind; to elicit a response
"The sad movie <u>evoked</u> tears from his mother."
evocation (n.), evocative (adj.)
evocare to call forth: *ex-* out of + *vocare* to call

invoke   **v.** to call upon in prayer or as a witness; to appeal to as an authority or in support of an argument
"Sailing home, Odysseus <u>invokes</u> Athena for protection."
invocation (n.)
invocare to call upon; to pray for: *in-* in; about + *vocare* to call

provoke   **v.** to incite to anger or resentment; to stir (someone else) to action or feeling; to annoy or anger deliberately
"Older brothers often <u>provoke</u> their younger brothers to demonstrate their superior power and control."
provocation (n.), provocative (adj.)
provocare to challenge; to provoke: *pro-* before; about + *vocare* to call

vocation   **n.** a person's employment or main occupation; a calling to a particular career or occupation (especially a "religious vocation")
"Her <u>vocation</u> was caring for others, whether as a mother and wife or in her job as a counselor."
vocative (adj.)
vocatio, vocationis calling < *vocare* to call

vociferous   **adj.** making, given to, or marked by noisy and vehement outcry
"The protesters expressed <u>vociferous</u> opposition to the state of emergency and the suspension of civil rights."
vociferari to exclaim; to shout: *vox, vocis* voice + *ferre* to carry

volition   **n.** one's own will; resolution
"Depression often expresses itself in low energy and lack of <u>volition</u>."
volitio, volitionis resolution < *volo* wish (present tense of *velle* to wish; to be willing)

voluntary   **adj.** done, given, or acting of one's own free will; working without payment
"We're not charging for admission, but your <u>voluntary</u> donation toward our

costs would be gratefully accepted."
voluntas will; desire; purpose

convolution   **n.** a rolled up or coiled state; one of the convex folds of the surface of the brain; a twisting together of various strands (abstract or concrete); a turn
"The convolutions in his logic led to erroneous results."
convolutus twisted; rolled up (past participle of *convolvere* to roll together; to twist: *con-* together + *volvere* to roll)

devolve   **v.** to pass on or delegate to another; to degenerate or deteriorate
"The fraternity party quickly devolved into an alcoholic orgy."
devolvere to roll down; to transfer: *de-* down; from + *volvere* to roll

evolve   **v.** to develop or achieve gradually
"The larva evolves into a chrysalis, from which a butterfly emerges."
evolution (n.), evolutionary (adj.)
evolvere to roll out; to unfold: *ex-* out + *volvere* to roll

revolve   **v.** to rotate around a central point or axis; to recur in cycles or periodically; to be centered on; to think over
"Over the course of a night, the constellations appear to revolve around the North Star."
revolution (n.)
revolvere to roll back or around: *re-* back + *volvere* to roll

voluble   talkative; fluent; turning easily on an axis; rotating
"A treasure house of neatly turned stories, my uncle was a voluble raconteur."
volubilis turning; rolling < *volvere* to roll

Exercise A

Fill in the blanks in the sentences below with the correct form of a word in the scroll above.

1. Some yogis have demonstrated _____ control over bodily functions that are normally considered involuntary.

2. He was _____ when he'd had a few drinks, but spoke very little when sober.

3. Her health and _____ made her very attractive, even though she was not especially pretty.

4. Before he was called to his current _____ as a Congregational minister, Rev. Dionne was a police officer.

5. The moderator tried to prevent the town meeting from _____ into a shouting match.

6. The medium pretended to _____ the spirits of the dead.

7. The skipper's mate left the lines coiled on the deck in a _____ of hemp.

8. In the _____ atmosphere of the party, he persuaded her to accept a laughing kiss under the mistletoe.

9. Staring at the smoking embers of a campfire _____ happy memories of my youth as a Boy Scout.

10. Since there is little money to be made in offering day trips, seasonal sailing is an _____ for most people.

11. Although the Marine was good at following orders, he floundered when asked to take initiative and act of his own _____.

12. There are numerous environmental groups that _____ for cleaner air and water.

13. Galileo argued that the Earth was not the center of the known universe and that the Sun did not _____ around it.

14. The _____ cheerleaders evoked an enthusiastic response from the spectators, who cheered the basketball team to victory.

15. One or two children in every class will try to _____ the teacher, but most kindergarten pupils try hard to behave.

16. The governor _____ a special panel to study ways to cut the budget.

17. People with severe diabetes cannot _____ without insulin.

18. His book _____ out of years of reporting on Synanon.

19. Some talk show hosts encourage _____ participation from their guests, to the point where three or four people are shouting at another and none of them can be heard clearly.

20. Darwin is remembered for arguing that, "In the struggle for _____, the fittest win out at the expense of their rivals because they succeed in adapting themselves best to their environment," a process he termed "natural selection."

Exercise B

Match the word with the letter of its definition.

1. ___ advocate
2. ___ avocation
3. ___ convivial
4. ___ convoke
5. ___ convolution
6. ___ devolve
7. ___ evoke
8. ___ evolve
9. ___ invoke
10. ___ provoke
11. ___ revolve
12. ___ survival
13. ___ survive
14. ___ vitality
15. ___ vivacious
16. ___ vocation
17. ___ vociferous
18. ___ volition
19. ___ voluble
20. ___ voluntary

a) lively
b) energy and wellbeing
c) to call upon in prayer or as a witness
d) the act or process of surviving; endurance
e) to bring or recall to the conscious mind
f) done, given, or acting of one's own free will
g) to call together an assembly or meeting
h) a hobby or minor occupation
i) to continue to live or exist; to outlast
j) speaking incessantly and fluently
k) to incite to anger or resentment
l) making a noisy and forceful outcry
m) to publicly recommend or support; to defend or act on behalf of
n) a coil or twist
o) to move in a circle around a central axis
p) sociable and enjoyable
q) to degenerate or deteriorate
r) one's own will; resolution or resolve
s) to develop or achieve gradually
t) a person's employment or main occupation; a religious calling

Exercise C

Solve the crossword puzzle.

Across
2 A person who publicly supports or recommends a particular cause or policy 4 To bring or recall to the conscious mind; to elicit a response 7 Talkative; fluent; turning easily on an axis; rotating 9 Full of animation and spirit; lively 10 To pass on or delegate to another; to degenerate or deteriorate 14 Fond of feasting, drinking, and good company; sociable 15 The act or process of remaining alive 16 A person's employment or main occupation 17 A rolled up or coiled state; a twisting together

Down
1 To call upon in prayer or as a witness 2 A hobby or minor occupation 3 To rotate around a central point or axis 5 To develop or achieve gradually 6 Done, given, or acting of one's own free will 8 To call together (an assembly or meeting) 9 Making, given to, or marked by noisy and vehement outcry 11 The capacity to live and grow; vigor or energy 12 One's own will; resolution 13 To incite to anger or resentment; to annoy or anger deliberately

Test 4

Choose the correct meaning for the underlined vocabulary word in each sentence.

1. "Doubtless the good man has spent many a studious hour in this old chair, either penning a sermon or reading some <u>abstruse</u> book of theology, till midnight came upon him unawares."
   Grandfather's Chair by Nathaniel Hawthorne

   (a) altruistic   (b) absolute   (c) obscure   (d) uncomplicated   (e) obsolete

2. "He did smile sometimes, it is true; and there was a good deal of dry, sarcastic humour about him, which told the more from the <u>imperturbable</u> gravity of his tone and manner."
   Typee by Herman Melville

   (a) unshakably calm   (b) understandable   (c) stubborn   (d) mocking   (e) anxious

3. "All John Reed's violent tyrannies, all his sisters' proud indifference, all his mother's aversion, all the servants' partiality, turned up in my disturbed mind like a dark deposit in a <u>turbid</u> well."
   Jane Eyre by Charlotte Bronte

   (a) deep   (b) pristine   (c) ceremonial   (d) dried out
   (e) muddy

4. "The frog that lived in the pond warned his friend to change his residence and entreated him to come and live with him, saying that he would enjoy greater safety from danger and more <u>abundant</u> food."
   Fables by Aesop

   (a) delectable   (b) plentiful   (c) scarce   (d) delicious   (e) favorable

5. "But at the <u>penultimate</u> word, Mary cried out with sharp reproof."
   The Valley of the Moon by Jack London

   (a) final   (b) sarcastic   (c) next to last   (d) blasphemous   (e) cruel

6. "It is no longer anything but a mass of sonorous vibrations incessantly sent forth from the numerous belfries; it floats, <u>undulates</u>, bounds, whirls over the city, and prolongs

far beyond the horizon the deafening circle of its oscillations."
Notre-Dame de Paris by Victor Hugo

(a) sings (b) rises and falls (c) breaks into action (d) becomes quiet (e) is submerged under water

7. "Unless you adopted the opinion of certain observers of the human heart, and thought that the chevalier had the voice of his nose, his organ of speech would have amazed you by its full and <u>redundant</u> sound."
An Old Maid by Honore de Balzac

(a) pusillanimous (b) superfluous (c) full-bodied (d) wavy (e) refined

8. "As a preface is the only place where an author can with propriety explain a purpose or apologize for shortcomings, I venture to <u>avail</u> myself of the privilege to make a statement for the benefit of my readers."
An Old-Fashioned Girl by Louisa May Alcott

(a) make use of (b) forswear (c) demur from (d) wallow in (e) humbly abide by

9. "Straight lines are too <u>prevalent</u> – too uninterruptedly continued – or clumsily interrupted at right angles."
Poems by Edgar Allan Poe

(a) confusing (b) superior in strength (c) commonly occurring (d) inflexible (e) capable of regeneration

10. "Again a startled look came over the somewhat <u>vacuous</u> face of Miss Mary Sutherland."
The Adventures of Sherlock Holmes by Sir Arthur Conan Doyle

(a) fruitless (b) conceited (c) vain (d) empty (e) kind

11. "Legally speaking, as well as morally speaking, it absolutely <u>vindicates</u> your husband's innocence."
Law and the Lady by Wilkie Collins

(a) clouds and obscures (b) ignores the evidence for (c) revives a claim (d) absolves and justifies (e) destroys absolutely

12. "With regard to narrow passes, if you can occupy them first, let them be strongly garrisoned and await the <u>advent</u> of the enemy."
The Art of War by Sun Tzu

(a) circumnavigation (b) battle cry (c) surrounding (d) enclosing
(e) approach

13. "A fortunate kick hurled Michael away and enabled the sailor to <u>intervene</u> once again with the mop."

    Michael, Brother of Jerry by Jack London

    (a) come together (b) come between (c) violate (d) come around
    (e) resume

14. "'They are all for you,' I pursued, addressing Miss Tita and carrying off this <u>veracious</u> statement by treating it as an innocent joke."

    The Aspern Papers by Henry James

    (a) honest (b) untrue (c) expressive (d) assertive (e) hungry

15. "He conceived Nature to be a woman with a deep <u>aversion</u> to tragedy."

    The Red Badge of Courage by Stephen Crane

    (a) complicity (b) opposition (c) loathing (d) affinity (e) warning

16. "By a <u>devious</u> track between the fields they wound back to the Starkfield road."

    Ethan Frome by Edith Wharton

    (a) series of spans (b) straight forward (c) turning aside (d) roundabout
    (e) abnormal

17. "But I thought that was perhaps no more than a natural reserve accentuated by the <u>verbose</u> frankness of her husband."

    Moon and Sixpence by W. Somerset Maugham

    (a) wordy (b) repetitive (c) crass (d) only words
    (e) overly familiar

18. "When he went downstairs, he rested his beak on the steps, lifted his right foot and then his left one; but his mistress feared that such feats would give him <u>vertigo</u>."

    A Simple Soul by Gustave Flaubert

    (a) backache (b) dizziness (c) clumsiness (d) pain (e) superior notions

19. "As a so eminently respectable man, Mr Podsnap was sensible of its being required of him to take <u>Providence</u> under his protection."

    Our Mutual Friend by Charles Dickens

    (a) happenstance (b) fate (c) divine direction (d) holy orders
    (e) venture

20. "Will you give the little maiden a potion, that she may possess the strength of twelve men, and vanquish the Snow Queen?"
Andersen's Fairy Tales by Hans Christian Andersen

(a) expel   (b) make visible   (c) observe   (d) conquer   (e) terrorize

21. "Athos read at a glance all these shades upon the visage of his faithful servant, and in the same tone he would have employed to speak to Raoul in his dream."
The Man in the Iron Mask by Alexandre Dumas

(a) countenance   (b) illusion   (c) foresight   (d) mental image
(e) peaceful demonstration

22. "Most of their dark forms were soon blended with the brown covering of the prairie; though the captives, who watched the slightest movement of their enemies with vigilant eyes, were now and then enabled to discern a human figure, drawn against the horizon, as some one, more eager than the rest, rose to his greatest height in order to extend the limits of his view."
The Prairie by James Fenimore Cooper

(a) unconquerable   (b) watchful   (c) vengeful   (d) furtive
(e) sleepy

23. "Not that I am an advocate for the prevailing fashion of acquiring a perfect knowledge of all languages, arts, and sciences."
Lady Susan by Jane Austen

(a) critic   (b) skeptic   (c) public supporter   (d) protester
(e) legal assistant

24. "Augustine, with his blue eyes and golden hair, his ethereally flexible form and vivacious features; and Alfred, dark-eyed, with haughty Roman profile, firmly-knit limbs, and decided bearing."
Uncle Tom's Cabin by Harriet Beecher Stowe

(a) friendly   (b) twisted   (c) handsome   (d) lively   (e) noble

25. "His words were re-echoed by the whole party, with vociferous cheers."
The Count of Monte Cristo by Alexandre Dumas

(a) noisy   (b) sloppy   (c) stirring   (d) prayerful   (e) drunken

Answer Key

Lesson I

Exercise A
1. immortal. 2. premonition. 3. commute. 4. mortify. 5. mores. 6. mortal. 7. permutations. 8. monitor. 9. morbid. 10. mortuary. 11. paramount. 12. admonish. 13. mutated. 14. moribund. 15. remonstrated. 16. muster. 17. morality. 18. mutable. 19. mountebank. 20. promontory.

Exercise B
1.g. 2.o. 3.k. 4.d. 5.n. 6.p. 7.f. 8.c. 9.q. 10.b. 11.h. 12.l. 13.e. 14.i. 15.r. 16.j. 17.a. 18.s. 19.m. 20.t.

Lesson II

Exercise A
1. innate. 2. nascent. 3. Native. 4 nativity. 5. prenatal. 6. Renaissance. 7. circumnavigate. 8. nave. 9. navigating. 10. navigation. 11. naval. 12. navy. 13. abnegate. 14. denigrate. 15. negated. 16. negation. 17. negative. 18. renegade. 19. renege. 20. enervate.

Exercise B
1.m. 2.g. 3.q. 4.d. 5.n. 6.h. 7.r. 8.c. 9.b. 10.a. 11.j. 12.e. 13.l. 14.o. 15.f. 16.t. 17.k. 18.p. 19.s. 20.i.

Lesson III

Exercise A
1. annihilate. 2. nihilism. 3. cognomens. 4. nomenclature. 5. nominal. 6. onomatopoeia. 7. renowned. 8. innovate. 9. innovation. 10. novas. 11. novelty. 12. novice. 13. renovate. 14. renovation. 15. nocturnes. 16. nocturnal. 17. announce. 18. annunciation. 19. renounce. 20. renunciation.

Exercise B
1.d. 2.l. 3.g. 4.o. 5.a. 6.m. 7.j. 8.q. 9.e. 10.r. 11.b. 12.t. 13.h. 14.p. 15.i. 16.n. 17.c. 18.f. 19.s. 20.k.

Lesson IV

Exercise A
1. ostensibly. 2. insubordinate. 3. orator. 4. ordinance. 5. ostentatious. 6. redolent. 7. inordinate. 8. orifice. 9. operate. 10. oculist. 11. olfactory. 12. ornaments. 13. oration. 14. orb. 15. oracle. 16. ordain. 17. odious. 18. orbit. 19. ornate.

Exercise B
1.g. 2.l. 3.c. 4.r. 5.m. 6.h. 7.i. 8.s. 9.q. 10.k. 11.e. 12.f. 13.o. 14.b. 15.d. 16.p. 17.j. 18.n. 19.a.

Lesson V

Exercise A
1. impassioned. 2. pecuniary. 3. patron. 4. passionate. 5. pacifist. 6. pastoral. 7. patrimony. 8. appease. 9. peccadilloes. 10. patriotism. 11. impassive. 12. repast. 13. pacify. 14. impeccable. 15. pallid. 16. paternity. 17. palliate. 18. patronized. 19. pall. 20. impecunious.

Exercise B
1.h. 2.o. 3.b. 4.i. 5.q. 6.m. 7.d. 8.k. 9.f. 10.e. 11.s. 12.a. 13.g. 14.r. 15.t. 16.j. 17.p. 18.l. 19.n. 20.c.

Lesson VI

Exercise A
1. pedestrian. 2. pending. 3. propeller. 4. pediment. 5. repelled. 6. expedient. 7. impending. 8. compel. 9. pedal. 10. expel. 11. penchant. 12. propensity. 13. impediment. 14. compulsion. 15. appendix. 16. pedometer. 17. pendant. 18. propelled. 19. expedite. 20. pedigree.

Exercise B
1.h. 2.i. 3.t. 4.r. 5.g. 6.d. 7.l. 8.o. 9.j. 10.s. 11.f. 12.c. 13.a. 14.e. 15.p. 16.k. 17.n. 18.b. 19.m. 20.q.

Lesson VII

Exercise A
1. placid. 2. implacable. 3. petition . 4. complaisant. 5. impious. 6. implicit. 7. pictographs. 8. appetite. 9. complicit. 10. competitor. 11. piety. 12. petulant. 13. depict. 14. duplicity. 15. compete. 16. placate. 17. expiate . 18. complacent. 19. pittance. 20. complicity.

Exercise B
1.m. 2.g. 3.j. 4.k. 5.s. 6.n. 7.b. 8.a. 9.q. 10.c. 11.e. 12.l. 13.t. 14.d. 15.f. 16.h. 17.r. 18.o. 19.i. 20.p.

Test 1

1. admonish	b. warn
2. immortal	d. enduring
3. moribund	a. near death
4. paramount	c. supreme
5. promontory	b. headland
6. circumnavigate	e. travel around
7. nascent	a. emerging
8. annihilate	c. destroy
9. Nihilism	d. denial of morality
10. nomenclature	b. terminology
11. nocturnal	e. nighttime
12. renown	a. fame

13. ostentatious   c. showy
14. olfactory   b. of smell
15. oracle   d. prophet
16. ornate   b. highly decorated
17. redolent   d. fragrant
18. appease   e. soothe
19. pallid   d. pale
20. pecuniary   c. financial
21. expedient   b. convenient
22. impediment   a. obstacle
23. complacent   c. self-satisfied
24. petulant   d. peevish
25. placate   e. pacify

Lesson VIII

Exercise A
1. portable. 2. interpose. 3. imponderable. 4. transpose. 5. export. 6. impose. 7. imposter. 8. superimpose. 9. pontificate . 10. exponent. 11. ponderous . 12. postpone. 13. deported. 14. deposed. 15. imports. 16. pontiff. 17. expose. 18. preponderant. 19. proponent. 20. rapport.
Exercise B
1.s. 2.l. 3.h. 4.o. 5.f. 6.d. 7.m. 8.p. 9.t. 10.c. 11.a. 12.b. 13.g. 14.e. 15.i. 16.j. 17.k. 18.q. 19.n. 20.r.

Lesson IX

Exercise A
1. reprisal. 2. express. 3. potential. 4. impress. 5. potable. 6. compress. 7. opportune. 8. depressed. 9. puissant. 10. impotent. 11. predatory. 12. oppressed. 13. potentate. 14. potion. 15. comprise. 16. opportunist. 17. reprehend. 18. depredate. 19. apprehended.
Exercise B
1.j. 2.o. 3.i. 4.e. 5.q. 6.r. 7.l. 8.d. 9.h. 10.s. 11.n. 12.m. 13.a. 14.f. 15.p. 16.c. 17.k. 18.b. 19.g.

Lesson X

Exercise A
1. punctilious. 2. pugilism. 3. compute. 4. punish. 5. approbation. 6. reputed. 7. impugned. 8. pugnacious. 9. puerile. 10. expunge. 11. computer. 12. putative. 13. reprobate. 14. punitive. 15. pungent. 16. compunction. 17. amputate. 18. reproved. 19. reputation. 20. impunity.
Exercise B
1.g. 2.p. 3.s. 4.d. 5.m. 6.j. 7.q. 8.a. 9.k. 10.r. 11.e. 12.o. 13.f. 14.n. 15.c. 16.i. 17.h. 18.b. 19.t. 20.l.

Lesson XI

Exercise A
1. incorrigible. 2. ridicule. 3. directive. 4. ratios. 5. regent. 6. rapture. 7. rationalize. 8.

rapacious. 9. insurgents. 10. rector. 11. deride. 12. arraign. 13. insurrection. 14. regular. 15. ridiculous. 16. rationale. 17. ravished. 18. rectify. 19. risible. 20. rational.
Exercise B
1.d. 2.l. 3.f. 4.o. 5.i. 6.a. 7.k. 8.r. 9.s. 10.p. 11.c. 12.m. 13.q. 14.h. 15.n. 16.t. 17.b. 18.e. 19.j. 20.g.

Lesson XII

Exercise A
1. rusticate. 2. derogatory. 3. disrupted/interrupted. 4. interrogative. 5. rotund. 6. abrogate. 7. interrupt/disrupt. 8. rogue. 9. rustic. 10. rotary. 11. arrogate. 12. rote. 13. rotunda. 14. interrogate. 15. rotate. 16. arrogant. 17. abrupt. 18. erupt. 19. prerogative. 20. ruptured
Exercise B
1.m. 2.e. 3.r. 4.s. 5.p. 6.h. 7.a. 8.q. 9.k. 10.o. 11.t. 12.n. 13.f. 14.d. 15.b. 16.i. 17.g. 18.j. 19.c. 20.l.

Lesson XIII

Exercise A
1. sanctity. 2. sagacious. 3. insult. 4. sacred. 5. assailed. 6. sanctimonious. 7. saline. 8. consecrate. 9. sapient. 10. sacrament. 11. assault. 12. sanction. 13. exults. 14. sacrilege. 15. sanguine. 16. execrate. 17. presaging. 18. sanctum. 19. sanctify. 20. consanguinity.
Exercise B
1.h. 2.l. 3.q. 4.b. 5.p. 6.r. 7.d. 8.o. 9.a. 10.s. 11.c. 12.i. 13.e. 14.f. 15.t. 16.k. 17.g. 18.n. 19.j. 20.m.

Lesson XIV

Exercise A
1. inscribed. 2. sequels. 3. dissecting. 4. subsequent. 5. scriptures. 6. scintilla. 7. consecutive. 8. segments. 9. proscribed. 10. manuscript. 11. subscribe. 12. prescribed. 13. satiate. 14. bisects. 15. ascribe. 16. transcribe. 17. consequences. 18. conscript. 19. sequence. 20. non sequitur.
Exercise B
1.f. 2.m. 3.h. 4.p. 5.l. 6.q. 7.b. 8.e. 9.t. 10.o. 11.s. 12.c. 13.r. 14.g. 15.n. 16.i. 17.j. 18.d. 19.a. 20.k.

Test 2

1. exponent — b. one who promotes an idea
2. interpose — c. introduce between things
3. ponderous — d. heavy
4. potable — b. drinkable
5. impotent — e. helpless
6. potentate — b. ruler
7. reprisal — a. retaliation
8. puissant — b. powerful

9. expunge — c. erase
10. impugn — a. challenge
11. puerile — d. childish
12. punctilious — b. meticulous
13. deride — a. ridicule
14. rapacious — b. voracious
15. rapture — e. ecstasy
16. abrogate — b. invalidate
17. prerogative — c. prerogative
18. rusticate — a. live in the country
19. assail — d. attack
20. presages — e. warnings
21. sagacious — a. prudent, shrewd
22. sanctimonious — b. morally superior
23. consecutive — c. sequential
24. satiate — d. fully satisfy
25. sequel — b. continuation

Lesson XV

Exercise A
1. session. 2. simultaneous. 3. sensory. 4. resent. 5. consensus. 6. sedentary. 7. simulate. 8. dissenting. 9. sensual. 10. assiduous. 11. dissimilar. 12. assented. 13. presentiment. 14. residual. 15. sedatives. 16. senile. 17. assimilated. 18. sentiment. 19. dissident. 20. simile.

Exercise B
1.m. 2.g. 3.k. 4.a. 5.t. 6.s. 7.j. 8.p. 9.q. 10.l. 11.d. 12.b. 13.i. 14.r. 15.f. 16.n. 17.h. 18.o. 19.e. 20.c.

Lesson XVI

Exercise A
1. solo. 2. sonic. 3. dissolve. 4. sonar. 5. soliloquy. 6. solvent. 7. dissolute. 8. Insomnia. 9. absolutely. 10. solitude. 11. resolve. 12. solute. 13. absolve. 14. somnolent. 15. resolution. 16. desolate. 17. unison. 18. solipsism. 19. resonate. 20. Supersonic.

Exercise B
1.h. 2.m. 3.p. 4.l. 5.j. 6.c. 7.n. 8.q. 9.i. 10.f. 11.t. 12.k. 13.b. 14.d. 15.r. 16.a. 17.g. 18.e. 19.o. 20.s.

Lesson XVII

Exercise A
1. circumspect. 2. spirited. 3. spectacle. 4. expire. 5. dispersed. 6. inspire. 7. perspective. 8. dispirited. 9. spectator. 10. aspersions. 11. conspiracy. 12. transpired. 13. introspective. 14. aspired. 15. specters. 16. despicable. 17. respiratory. 18. specimen. 19. spiritual. 20. spectrum.

Exercise B
1.g. 2.f. 3.m. 4.t. 5.n. 6.k. 7.j. 8.p. 9.d. 10.q. 11.h. 12.e. 13.c. 14.o. 15.r. 16.a. 17.l. 18.b. 19.s.

20. i.

Lesson XVIII

Exercise A
1. sumptuous. 2. Strait. 3. constellation. 4. assuage. 5. obstruct. 6. constrain. 7. constant. 8. stringent. 9. construe. 10. ousted. 11. constrict. 12. suave. 13. stellar. 14. construct. 15. destitute. 16. instruct. 17. astringent. 18. presume. 19. restitution. 20. subsume.

Exercise B
1.i. 2.m. 3.p. 4.h. 5.o. 6.d. 7.r. 8.b. 9.n. 10.l. 11.g. 12.t. 13.k. 14.a. 15.s. 16.c. 17.q. 18.e. 19.f. 20.j.

Lesson XIX

Exercise A
1. temporal. 2. temperance. 3. contemporary. 4. contingent. 5. temperament. 6. tempest. 7. tangible. 8. contiguous. 9. extemporaneous. 10. tactile. 11. tempo. 12. temerity. 13. tact. 14. temperate. 15. temper. 16. tangents. 17. intangibles. 18. tempered. 19. temerarious. 20. temporize.

Exercise B
1.g. 2.m. 3.p. 4.a. 5.r. 6.i. 7.b. 8.j. 9.c. 10.o. 11.d. 12.s. 13.e. 14.q. 15.t. 16.f. 17.n. 18.h. 19.k. 20.l.

Lesson XX

Exercise A
1. tenure. 2. Mediterranean. 3. detained. 4. retentive. 5. Terrestrial. 6. terrain. 7. interminable. 8. contain. 9. retain. 10. inter. 11. pertinacious. 12. tenacious. 13. pertain. 14. tenable. 15. subterranean. 16. terminate. 17. impertinent. 18. pertinent. 19. extraterrestrial. 20. terracotta.

Exercise B
1.f. 2.m. 3.d. 4.n. 5.p. 6.l. 7.q. 8.c. 9.o. 10.b. 11.h. 12.g. 13.i. 14.s. 15.j. 16.a. 17.t. 18.e. 19.k. 20.r.

Test 3

1. assiduous — c. showing great care
2. assimilate — a. absorb
3. presentiment — b. premonition
4. sedentary — d. sitting
5. simile — b. figure of speech
6. absolve — c. free
7. dissolute — d. unrestrained, debauched
8. insomnia — a. sleeplessness
9. soliloquy — c. monologue
10. unison — e. at the same time
11. aspersion — d. insult
12. dispirits — b. discourages

193

13. perspective — a. point of view
14. spectrum — c. range of light values
15. assuage — b. decrease
16. oust — d. eject
17. stringent — b. rigorous
18. sumptuous — d. lavish
19. contiguous — c. adjacent
20. extemporaneous — b. impromptu
21. temporal — d. earthly
22. impertinent — a. impolite
23. interminable — b. endless
24. retentive — c. able to hold
25. tenure — a. term

Lesson XXI

Exercise A
1. protruding. 2. distract. 3. obtrude. 4. contort. 5. abstruse. 6. torsion. 7. extract. 8. turbid. 9. detracted. 10. context. 11. extrude. 12. tortuous. 13. pretext. 14. retort. 15. imperturbable. 16. totalitarian. 17. distorts. 18. intrude. 19. intractable. 20. torque.

Exercise B
1.p. 2.t. 3.q. 4.m. 5.i. 6.s. 7.k. 8.e. 9.d. 10.r. 11.g. 12.c. 13.a. 14.o. 15.h. 16.b. 17.n. 18.f. 19.l. 20.j.

Lesson XXII

Exercise A
1. abound. 2. undulating. 3. rupture. 4. ultimate. 5. undulate. 6. disrupt. 7. abundant. 8. penultimate. 9. uxorious. 10. interrupt. 11. urbane. 12. abrupt. 13. inundated. 14. erupt. 15. corrupt. 16. redundant. 17. suburban. 18. ultimatum. 19. urban. 20. redound.

Exercise B
1.f. 2.i. 3.a. 4.l. 5.m. 6.h. 7.b. 8.p. 9.s. 10.d. 11.c. 12.r. 13.g. 14.q. 15.o. 16.k. 17.n. 18.j. 19.t. 20.e.

Lesson XXIII

Exercise A
1. valor. 2. invasion. 3. prevalent. 4. evade. 5. vindictive. 6. vacant. 7. pervasive. 8. invaded. 9. vindicate. 10. vacuous. 11. availed. 12. vaunt. 13. evacuate. 14. vendetta. 15. convalesce. 16. vain. 17. pervaded. 18. evasive. 19. prevail. 20. vanity.

Exercise B
1.p. 2.k. 3.g. 4.r. 5.o. 6.i. 7.q. 8.d. 9.c. 10.b. 11.l. 12.s. 13.f. 14.e. 15.n. 16.j. 17.m. 18.a. 19.t. 20.h.

Lesson XXIV

Exercise A
1. event. 2. verify. 3. averred. 4. intervene. 5. circumvent. 6. verisimilitude. 7. convention. 8. veracity. 9. venue. 10. advent. 11. ventilate. 12. veracious. 13. convene. 14. verity. 15. prevent. 16. convenience. 17. contravene. 18. vent. 19. preventive. 20. veritable.
Exercise B
1.t. 2.m. 3.k. 4.o. 5.g. 6.f. 7.n. 8.a. 9.b. 10.e. 11.l. 12.i. 13.q. 14.d. 15.p. 16.r. 17.s. 18.j. 19.h. 20.c.

Lesson XXV

Exercise A
1. revert. 2. pervert. 3. deviate. 4. viaduct. 5. aversion. 6. avert. 7. divert. 8. versatile. 9. verbal. 10. devious. 11. convert. 12. deviation. 13. verbose. 14. vertigo. 15. adversity. 16. controversy. 17. verbatim. 18. diversion. 19. introvert. 20. adverse.
Exercise B
1.h. 2.c. 3.k. 4.n. 5.o. 6.d. 7.j. 8.m. 9.b. 10.g. 11.i. 12.a. 13.t. 14.l. 15.s. 16.f. 17.q. 18.r. 19.e. 20.p.

Lesson XXVI

Exercise A
1. invisible. 2. surveillance. 3. visage. 4. providence. 5. vanquish. 6. visualize. 7. evident. 8. visibility. 9. vigil. 10. visionary. 11. envision. 12. evict. 13. evidence. 14. vigilant. 15. Victory. 16. improvise. 17. Visual. 18. invincible. 19. revise. 20. supervising.
Exercise B
1.k. 2.g. 3.t. 4.m. 5.d. 6.p. 7.j. 8.q. 9.n. 10.b. 11.f. 12.r. 13.c. 14.a. 15.h. 16.s. 17.e. 18.o. 19.l. 20.i.

Lesson XXVII

Exercise A
1. voluntary. 2. voluble. 3. vitality. 4. vocation. 5. devolving. 6. invoke. 7. convolution. 8. convivial. 9. evokes. 10. avocation. 11. volition. 12. advocate. 13. revolve. 14. vivacious. 15. provoke. 16. convoke. 17. survive. 18. evolved. 19. vociferous. 20. survival.
Exercise B
1.   2.h. 3.p. 4.g. 5.n. 6.q. 7.e. 8.s. 9.c. 10.k. 11.o. 12.d. 13.i. 14.b. 15.a. 16.t. 17.l. 18.r. 19.j. 20.f.

Test 4

1. abstruse — c. obscure
2. imperturbable — a. unshakably calm
3. turbid — e. muddy
4. abundant — b. plentiful
5. penultimate — c. next to last
6. undulates — b. rises and falls

7. redundant — b. superfluous, repetitive
8. avail — a. make use of
9. prevalent — c. commonly occurring
10. vacuous — d. empty
11. vindicates — d. absolves and justifies
12. advent — e. approach
13. intervene — b. come between
14. veracious — a. honest
15. aversion — c. loathing
16. devious — d. roundabout
17. verbose — a. wordy
18. vertigo — b. dizziness
19. Providence — c. divine direction
20. vanquish — d. conquer
21. visage — a. countenance
22. vigilant — b. watchful
23. advocate — c. supporter
24. vivacious — d. lively
25. vociferous — a. noisy

INDEX

abnegate, 15
abound, 148
abrogate, 79
abrupt, 80
abrupt, 147
absolute, 108
absolve, 108
abstruse, 143
abundant, 148
admonish, 7
advent, 159
adverse, 166
adversity, 166
advocate, 178
amputate, 68
annihilate, 20
announce, 22
annunciation, 22
appease, 33
appendix, 40
appetite, 45
apprehend, 62
approbation, 67
arraign, 73
arrogant, 79
arrogate, 79
ascribe, 91
aspersion, 113
aspire, 114
assail, 86
assault, 86
assent, 102
assiduous, 101
assimilate, 103
assuage, 121

astringent, 120
avail, 154
aver, 160
aversion, 167
avert, 167
avocation, 179
bisect, 92
circumnavigate, 15
circumspect, 113
circumvent, 159
cognomen, 20
commute, 10
compel, 39
compete, 45
competitor, 45
complacent, 46
complaisant, 46
complicit, 47
complicity, 47
compress, 63
comprise, 62
compulsion, 39
compunction, 68
compute, 68
computer, 69
consanguinity, 87
conscript, 91
consecrate, 85
consecutive, 93
consensus, 102
consequence, 93
conspiracy, 114
constant, 119
constellation, 120
constrain, 120

constrict, 120
construct, 120
construe, 120
contain, 131
contemporary, 127
context, 141
contiguous, 125
contingent, 125
contort, 141
contravene, 159
controversy, 167
convalesce, 154
convene, 159
convenience, 159
convention, 160
convert, 167
convivial, 178
convoke, 179
convolution, 180
corrupt, 147
denigrate, 15
depict, 46
deport, 57
depose, 55
depredate, 62
depressed, 63
deride, 75
derogatory, 79
desolate, 107
despicable, 113
destitute, 119
detain, 131
detract, 142
deviate, 168
deviation, 168

197

devious, 168
devolve, 180
directive, 74
disperse, 113
dispirit, 114
disrupt, 80
disrupt, 147
dissect, 92
dissent, 102
dissident, 101
dissimilar, 103
dissolute, 108
dissolve, 108
distort, 142
distract, 142
diversion, 167
divert, 167
duplicity, 47
enervate, 16
envision, 172
erupt, 81
erupt, 147
evacuate, 153
evade, 154
evasive, 154
event, 160
evict, 174
evidence, 172
evident, 172
evoke, 179
evolve, 180
execrate, 85
expedient, 40
expedite, 40
expel, 39
expiate, 46
expire, 114
exponent, 55
export, 57
expose, 55
express, 63
expunge, 68
extemporaneous, 127
extract, 143
extraterrestrial, 132
extrude, 143

exult, 87
immortal, 8
impassioned, 34
impassive, 34
impeccable, 35
impecunious, 35
impediment, 40
impending, 40
impertinent, 131
imperturbable, 143
impious, 46
implacable, 46
implicit, 47
imponderable, 56
import, 57
impose, 55
imposter, 56
impotent, 61
impress, 63
improvise, 172
impugn, 67
impunity, 68
incorrigible, 74
innate, 15
innovate, 21
innovation, 21
inordinate, 28
inscribe, 91
insomnia, 109
inspire, 114
instruct, 121
insubordinate, 28
insult, 87
insurgent, 74
insurrection, 74
intangible, 125
inter, 132
interminable, 132
interpose, 56
interrogate, 79
interrogative, 80
interrupt, 81
interrupt, 148
intervene, 160
intractable, 143
introspective, 113

introvert, 167
intrude, 143
inundate, 148
invade, 154
invasion, 154
invincible, 174
invisible, 172
invoke, 179
manuscript, 92
mediterranean, 133
monitor, 7
morality, 8
morbid, 8
mores, 8
moribund, 8
mortal, 8
mortify, 10
mortuary, 10
mountebank, 7
muster, 8
mutable, 10
mutate, 10
nascent, 14
native, 14
nativity, 14
naval, 15
nave, 15
navigate, 15
navigation, 15
navy, 15
negate, 15
negation, 16
negative, 16
nihilism, 20
nocturnal, 22
nocturne, 22
nomenclature, 20
nominal, 21
non sequitur, 93
nova, 21
novelty, 21
novice, 21
obstruct, 121
obtrude, 143
oculist, 27
odious, 27

olfactory, 27
onomatopoeia, 21
operate, 28
opportune, 61
opportunist, 61
oppress, 63
oracle, 28
oration, 28
orator, 28
orb, 28
orbit, 28
ordain, 28
ordinance, 29
orifice, 28
ornament, 29
ornate, 29
ostensible, 29
ostentatious, 29
oust, 119
pacifist, 33
pacify, 33
pall, 33
palliate, 34
pallid, 34
paramount, 8
passionate, 34
pastoral, 34
paternity, 34
patrimony, 34
patriotism, 34
patron, 34
patronize, 35
peccadillo, 35
pecuniary, 35
pedal, 40
pedestrian, 40
pedigree, 41
pediment, 40
pedometer, 41
penchant, 40
pendant, 40
pending, 40
penultimate, 148
permutation, 10
perspective, 113
pertain, 131

pertinacious, 131
pertinent, 132
pervade, 154
pervasive, 154
pervert, 167
petition, 45
petulant, 45
pictograph, 46
piety, 46
pittance, 46
placate, 47
placid, 47
ponderous, 56
pontiff, 56
pontificate, 56
portable, 57
postpone, 56
potable, 62
potentate, 61
potential, 62
potion, 62
predatory, 62
premonition, 7
prenatal, 14
preponderant, 56
prerogative, 80
presage, 86
prescribe, 92
presentiment, 102
presume, 121
pretext, 141
prevail, 154
prevalent, 155
prevent, 160
preventive, 160
promontory, 8
propel, 39
propeller, 39
propensity, 40
proponent, 56
proscribe, 92
protrude, 143
providence, 173
provoke, 179
puerile, 67
pugilism, 68

pugnacious, 68
puissant, 62
punctilious, 68
pungent, 68
punish, 68
punitive, 68
putative, 69
rapacious, 73
rapport, 57
rapture, 73
ratio, 73
rational, 74
rationale, 74
rationalize, 74
ravish, 73
rectify, 74
rector, 75
redolent, 27
redound, 149
redundant, 149
regent, 75
regular, 74
remonstrate, 8
renaissance, 14
renegade, 16
renege, 16
renounce, 22
renovate, 21
renovation, 22
renowned, 21
renunciation, 22
repast, 34
repel, 39
reprehend, 62
reprisal, 62
reprobate, 67
reprove, 67
reputation, 69
reputed, 69
resent, 102
residual, 101
resolution, 108
resolve, 108
resonate, 109
respiratory, 115
restitution, 119

retain, 132
retentive, 132
retort, 142
revert, 167
revise, 173
revolve, 180
ridicule, 75
ridiculous, 75
risible, 75
rogue, 80
rotary, 80
rotate, 80
rote, 80
rotund, 80
rotunda, 80
rupture, 81
rupture, 148
rustic, 81
rusticate, 81
sacrament, 85
sacred, 85
sacrilege, 85
sagacious, 86
saline, 87
sanctify, 86
sanctimonious, 86
sanction, 86
sanctity, 86
sanctum, 86
sanguine, 87
sapient, 86
satiate, 91
scintilla, 91
scripture, 92
sedative, 101
sedentary, 101
segment, 92
senile, 102
sensory, 102
sensual, 102
sentiment, 103
sequel, 93
sequence, 93
session, 102
simile, 103
simulate, 103

simultaneous, 103
soliloquy, 107
solipsism, 107
solitude, 107
solo, 107
solute, 108
solvent, 108
somnolent, 109
sonar, 109
sonic, 109
specimen, 114
spectacle, 114
spectator, 114
specter, 114
spectrum, 114
spirited, 115
spiritual, 115
stellar, 120
strait, 120
stringent, 120
suave, 121
subscribe, 92
subsequent, 93
subsume, 121
subterranean, 133
suburban, 149
sumptuous, 121
superimpose, 56
supersonic, 109
supervise, 173
surveillance, 173
survival, 178
survive, 178
tact, 125
tactile, 126
tangent, 126
tangible, 126
temerarious, 126
temerity, 126
temper , 126
temperament, 126
temperance, 126
temperate, 126
tempered, 127
tempest, 127
tempo , 127

temporal, 127
temporize, 127
tenable, 132
tenacious, 132
tenure, 132
terminate, 132
terracotta, 133
terrain, 133
terrestrial, 133
torque, 142
torsion, 142
tortuous, 142
totalitarian, 142
transcribe, 92
transpire, 115
transpose, 56
turbid, 143
ultimate, 148
ultimatum, 148
undulate, 149
undulating, 149
unison, 109
urban, 149
urbane, 149
uxorious, 149
vacant, 153
vacuous, 153
vain, 153
valor, 155
vanity, 153
vanquish, 174
vaunt, 154
vendetta, 155
vent, 160
ventilate, 160
venue, 160
veracious, 161
veracity, 161
verbal, 166
verbatim, 166
verbose, 166
verify, 161
verisimilitude, 161
veritable, 161
verity, 161
versatile, 168

vertigo, 168
viaduct, 168
victory, 174
vigil, 173
vigilant, 173
vindicate, 155
vindictive, 155

visage, 173
visibility, 173
visionary, 173
visual, 173
visualize, 177
vitality, 178
vivacious, 178

vocation, 179
vociferous, 179
volition, 179
voluble, 180
voluntary, 179
voracious, 161

www.ingramcontent.com/pod-product-compliance
Lightning Source LLC
Chambersburg PA
CBHW060314240426
43661CB00059B/2759